PRAYER AGAINST

WITCHCRAFT DREAM

AND

STORM OF DARKNESS

TELLA OLAYERI

08023583168

Published By:

GOD'S LINK VENTURES

Email tellaolayeri@gmail.com

Website www.tellaolayeri.com

US Contact
Ruth Jack
14 Milewood Road
Verbank
N.Y.12585
U.S.A. +19176428989

DEDICATION

This book is dedicated to the **HOLY GHOST** for inspiring me to write this eye opener book.

APPRECIATION

My appreciation goes to my dedicated wife, **MRS NGOZI OLAYERI,** who typed the manuscript of this book and design the cover page.

My darling wife I say thank you. My appreciation equally goes to my lovely children, **MISS IBUKUN, DAVID, MICHAEL, COMFORT and MERCY.** They encouraged me day and night as I write this book. Hurray, after seven years of research, reading, listening to counsels and support of the Holy Spirit etc. the long awaited book, bad dream enemies use to rob blessing and the way out is out!

Respect and honor should be given to who is due. Favor comes from God and men as well. My calling (writing evangelism) met the timely support of a particular man of God, preacher, teacher, prophet and General Overseer. He awakes my inner man, gave me sound spiritual support and stood by me in fulfillment of my calling.
This book you are holding is a testimony of my claim. This book wouldn't have seen the light of the day, if not for the spiritual encouragement I gathered from my father in the Lord who served as

spiritual mirror that brightens my hope to explore my calling.

I am talking of no any other person than the **General Overseer of *MOUNTAIN OF FIRE AND MIRACLES MINISTRIES WORLD WIDE*, DR. D. K. OLUKOYA.**

Once again, I say thank you sir. Your support has yielded yet another earth shaking book.

THANKS

Evangelist Tella Olayeri.

HOW TO USE THIS BOOK

Prayers are written at the end of each chapter of this book. You can as well raise prayer points to address your dream situation as the spirit directs you.

It is good you cancel every bad dream as soon as you wake from sleep, as delay may be dangerous. Whenever you dream good dreams, pray for its manifestation. Do not wait for answer; rather work towards its actualization. Manifestation is not automatic. Sometimes, for security reasons don't share your dream with people anyhow. Let your dream materialize first, so that it is not countered by people you discuss it with.

Endeavor to do night vigil with this book using prayer points written at the end of each chapter, and or, any prayer book you know will address your situation. Let your vigil start around 12 midnights and pray for two to three hours. If you are facing strong challenges, I advise you go for two or three days dry fasting, taking warm water, (not hot tea!), to clear your throat from drying. Do this, and be ready for quick answer to your petitions.

PREFACE

Enough is enough; bad dream must not be given breathing space in your life. It is bad to be molested with bad dreams. The heart beats and bleeds. Bad dreams introduce fear to life. Heart break and attack becomes the order of the day. What a good thing if we can address and overcome bad dreams.

We must arise as gallant soldiers in Christ and in prayer to subdue and cancel bad dreams. Torments of bad dream are enormous. It breaks heart and cause undue fear. How do you imagine being crushed in the dream, fed in the dream, be a slave in the dream, or being pressed down in the dream? You feel unsafe with multiple sorrows if you can't interpret dreams.

To all bad dreams, there is an answer. It is either you pray against it, warned in the dream or look for right step to take in order to stop it. This book is loaded with right answer to all these. The step you take will restore whatever you lost in the dream and bring you to a state of enough is enough.

This book shall address every legal ground enemy is using to torment and inflict your life, with pains and trouble. By the verdict of the court of heaven, it shall be declared null and void, and you shall be discharged and acquitted from all legal ground working against you.

No matter what, bad dream shall not enslave you, or put your life in reverse gear. Wake up unto Christ and be a winner!

GOOD NEWS!!!

My audiobook is now available, to get one visit acx.com and search **"Tella Olayeri."**

Brethren, to be loaded and reloaded visit: *amazon.com/author/tellaolayeri* for a full spiritual sojourn for my books.

Thanks.

PREVIOUS PUBLICATIONS OF THE AUTHOR

1. <u>100% CONFESSIONS and PROPHECIES to Locate Helpers and helpers to locate you</u>
2. <u>1000 Prayer Points for Children Breakthrough</u>
3. <u>1010 (One Thousand and Ten) DREAMS and Interpretations</u>
4. <u>2000 Dangerous Prayer for First Born</u>
5. <u>365 DREAMS and INTERPRETATIONS</u>
6. <u>430 Prayers to Cancel Bad Dreams and Overcome Witchcraft Powers part one (DREAMS AND YOU Book 1)</u>
7. <u>430 Prayers to Claim Good Dreams and Overcome Witchcraft Powers part two (DREAMS AND YOU Book 2)</u>
8. <u>630 Acidic Prayers: With Missile Prayer for Speedy Breakthrough, Healing and Deliverance</u>
9. <u>650 DREAMS AND INTERPRETATIONS</u>
10. <u>700 Prayers to Clear Unemployment Out of Your Way</u>
11. <u>720 Missile Prayers that Silence Enemies: Prayers that Bring Peace and Rest</u>
12. <u>740 Rocket Prayers that Break Satanic Embargo</u>
13. <u>777 Deliverance Prayers for Healing and Breakthrough</u>
14. <u>800 Deliverance Prayer for Middle Born: Daily Devotional for Teen and Adult</u>

See all at: amazon.com/author/tellaolayeri

Table of Contents

CHAPTER 1

IF YOU BATH WITH DIRTY WATER IN THE DREAM

In the spirit, tragedy strikes only on the mature day set aside by Satan. Satanic calendar is well arranged by powers of darkness to cause havoc at prescribed day or date in the life of a victim. Thus, tragedy strikes not at once, but pre-arranged. It is a disaster if you have premonition of this but don't take it serious or you don't know the meaning of the dream. At times when it is dawn on you, you are taken aback of what happen in the past, the terrible dreams and non-challant attitude to it. What we should realize is, tragedy doesn't come over night, it happens first in the spirit. No wonder, it is said, "The spirit controls the physical".

To bath with dirty water in the dream foretells, there is a particular power at the corridor of your life that wants to pollute, disgrace or baptize you with poverty. Pollution is the architect of hatred and ill-luck. A dream of this nature warns of who you mix with, and a warning to keep your secret to yourself. Out of jealousy, those you trusted may attack you in the spirit with arrow of pollution and failure.

Enemies are loaded with spiritual recklessness to attack, naked and destroy destinies. They are notorious, faceless and wicked. They don't want good things of life for people, but prefer to overheat and trouble their destiny.

If you are seen from afar and you are hated by people, know that there is pollution in your body. When you are in the midst of people, but you are singled out as bad, pollution is heating you badly. So, if you bath with dirty water in the dream, you are most likely to experience hatred, ill-luck, failure and setback.

THE WAY OUT

1. Pray for anointing oil of God to flow in your life from your head to your toe, to cleanse your impurity.
2. Pray and pull down every barrier and obstacle that lie on your way
3. Be a born again Christian. Ask for forgiveness of sin and quit sin

4. Be a prayer warrior whose prayer turns life around. Let your prayer ignite riot in the kingdom of Satan

5. Check your attitude and be a winner. Build good character that wiil attracts helpers to you.

6. Read the Bible, it is the root of facts, wisdom and power that enlarge coast of living. If you read your bible and apply the Word, Satan is will be silenced, while enemies of your soul shall scatter.

7. Avoid temptation that pollutes soul and body. If you don't want to trade with the devil, stay out of his shop.

8. Avoid worldly things. A worldly Christian is spiritually diseased. Worldly things make gold their god; saints make God their gold

9. Avoid swimming in ocean of lust. Be in the spirit, let God guide you, and lead your step out of dirty things.

10. Read good Christian books that give wisdom, power and excellence. The more you read good books better it is for you.

11. In a situation like this, I recommend you go for deliverance in a living church that belief in deliverance prayer

12. Cleanse yourself with blood of Jesus. Soak yourself in the pool blood of Jesus, and

command every impurity in your life to expire
and die.

BIBLICAL GUIDELINE

1. Bible Reading: 2 Kings 5
2. Bible Reference: John 5:5-6

   5. . ***"And a certain man was there, which had
   an infirmity thirty and eight years.***
   ***6. When Jesus saw him lie, and knew that
   he had been now a long time in that case,
   he saith unto him, will thou be made
   whole?"***

   6. Positive confession: Exodus 23:25
   ***"And ye shall serve the LORD your God,
   and he shall bless thy bread, and thy water,
   and I will take sickness away from the
   midst of thee"***

3. Champion prayer: Blood of Jesus, cleanse me
   of pollution in the name of Jesus. Amen
4. Fasting: 6am-6pm
5. Time of Prayer: 12pm – 3am
6. Duration of prayer: 7 days fasting and prayer

PRAYER POINTS

1. O Lord, let my prayer ignite fire in the Kingdom of Satan, in the name of Jesus
2. O Lord, let my prayer ignite riot, in the kingdom of Satan, in the name of Jesus
3. O Lord, let my prayer ignite thunder, in the kingdom of Satan, in the name of Jesus
4. O Lord, forgive me sins that will not allow my prayer to get answer, in the name of Jesus
5. Every barrier on my way to success give way, in the name of Jesus
6. I break and scatter barriers militating against my success, in the name of Jesus
7. O Lord, make me whole, in the name of Jesus
8. Every pollution in my body, expire in the name of Jesus
9. Any power assign to naked me, run mad and die in the name of Jesus
10. Spiritual recklessness against me, be silenced, in the name of Jesus
11. Any power assign to scatter my destiny, die in the name of Jesus
12. Powers that sponsor rejection in my life, die in the name of Jesus
13. Every arrow of prayerlessness fired against me backfire, in the name of Jesus
14. Every arrow of infirmity fired against my life, backfire in the name of Jesus

15. Every arrow of hatred fired against me, backfire in the name of Jesus

16. Every arrow of ill-luck fired against me, backfire in the name of Jesus

17. Every arrow of failure fired against me, backfire in the name of Jesus

18. Every arrow of setback fired against me, backfire in the name of Jesus

19. Tragedy waiting for maturity day in my life, die in the name of Jesus

20. Satanic calendar for my life, catch fire and roast to ashes in the name of Jesus

21. Every power of darkness in the corridor of my life, assign to pollute me die in the name of Jesus

22. Every power of darkness in the corridor of my life, assign to disgrace me die, in the name of Jesus

23. Every power of darkness in the corridor of my life, assign to fire me with water of poverty die

24. Every wickedness of the wicked against my destiny, scatter in the name of Jesus

25. Rivers of problem flowing into my life, dry up by fire in the name of Jesus

26. Heal me O Lord from every sickness in the spirit

27. O Lord, break every link I have with poverty, in the name of Jesus
28. Every void caused by pollution in my life, I fill you with success, in the name of Jesus
29. Every void caused by pollution in my life, I fill you with joy, in the name of Jesus
30. Every void caused by pollution in my life, I fill you with favour and mercy of God
31. Every void caused by pollution in my life, I fill you with testimony in the name of Jesus
32. Those I discuss my issues with and are now attacking me, meet double failure
33. Holy Ghost, padlock my mouth from revealing my secrets to enemy
34. O Lord, direct my step to right people to mix with in the name of Jesus
35. O Lord, give me wisdom to handle situation as it arises, in the name of Jesus
36. O Lord, give me power to forge ahead in life, in the name of Jesus
37. O Lord, build me with character that invite helpers, in the name of Jesus
38. O Lord, enlarge my coast by fire in the name of Jesus
39. From afar shall people see and love me in the name of Jesus

40. Shop of Satan inviting me for disgrace, catch fire and roast to ashes, in the name of Jesus

41. I reverse my steps from shop of Satan, in the name of Jesus

42. Satan, leave me alone I shall not dwell in your shop, in the name of Jesus

43. O Lord my God, bless the bread in my hand, in the name of Jesus

44. O Lord my God, bless the water I shall drink and use, in the name of Jesus

45. I soak myself in the pool blood of Jesus and receive liberty from powers of darkness

46. I wash myself with blood of Jesus

47. I drink blood of Jesus against impurity in the name of Jesus

48. I silence action of the enemy against me by the power in the blood of Jesus

49. Every impurity in my body, be cleansed with blood of Jesus

50. Anointing of God, flow from my head to my toes for breakthrough in the name of Jesus

51. My breakthrough, appear by fire, in the name of Jesus

52. O Lord, take sickness away from me, in the name of Jesus

53. I shall not romance temptations that will pollute my body in the name of Jesus

54. I shall not romance temptations that will pollute my soul in the name of Jesus
55. I shall not swim in polluted water, in the name of Jesus
56. I shall not bath with polluted water, in the name of Jesus
57. Spirit of excellence dwell in my life, in the name of Jesus
58. I am delivered from evil pollution, in the name of Jesus
59. O Lord, lead my steps out of dirty water in the name of Jesus
60. I shall not make gold my god, in the name of Jesus
61. O Lord, make me a saint that make God his gold, in the name of Jesus
62. O Lord, let me be heavenly minded, as against being worldly minded, in the name of Jesus
63. O God arise, put my enemy to shame, in the name of Jesus
64. I shall not be cited as a bad example, in the multitude of people in the name of Jesus
65. Surplus favour shall over ride my failure, in the name of Jesus
66. O Lord, let root of witchcraft in my life wither, in the name of Jesus

67. No dark water shall control my destiny, in the name of Jesus

68. Praise the Lord, every impossibility in my life shall disappear in the name of Jesus

CHAPTER 2

IF YOU DREAM OF A SHABBY, DIRTY OR ROUGH BOOKSHELF

Danger lurk around in every life, be it at young or old age. Enemies are bent at doing evil. They are wicked masters and slave dragons; trouble shooters that abuse and injure rights of innocent in the sleep. They are wicked monitoring powers that ensure you suffer trespass and transgression in your dream.

What is the meaning of, to dream of a shabby, dirty or rough bookshelf? Spiritually, it is a dream that foretells danger, ahead. It suggests you may experience academic setback, career difficulty, and or, poor attitude of handling evangelism. Thus, it suggests you are spiritually oppressed, or you allow it happen.

Satan's calculation is to make you sad all times. To your children, he wants them to fail, to you he doesn't want to read, do research or enjoy academic exposure. Satan wants you to graduate from one problem to another. He wants you to swim and dine in agony. Satan doesn't want you to pray or be on your knee to praise God or pray, because he has no one he prays to. For this reason, he hates evangelism, the spread of the Word or gathering of the saints. To achieve this, he attacks you and the church through dream. Such attack makes you dream horrible dream of this nature.

THE WAY OUT

1. As a minister of God, be focused in your ministry. Evangelize for God. As soldier follows his general, as the servant follows his master, as scholar follows his teacher, as sheep follows his shepherd, so you should follow Christ and do his work.
2. Don't dose in pastoral calling. The job of a pastor is to gather the people in the arms and draw them nearer to God.
3. Be a gallant preacher, you must be a soldier and a shepherded.
4. Cover your property, destiny and career with blood of Jesus.
5. Fire back every evil arrow fired against you.
6. Call your God to lift every embargo placed upon you.
7. Cleanse your bookshelf with spiritual insecticide and use divine broom to cleanse your spiritual cupboard.
8. Embrace Jesus, believe in him and surrender to him. Hence, be a born again Christian. No

physician like the Lord, no tonic like his promise, no wine like his love.

9. Read your Bible and study it, know it and practice it.

10. Let your dreams be important in your spiritual race. Belief in dreams, address it with all seriousness.

11. Read good Christian books that promote spiritual awareness.

12. Be a born again Christian and surrender your life to Christ.

13. Pray without ceasing. Prayer for open good doors, and close bad door of Satan.

14. Pray for mercy of God and of men to shine and abide in you.

BIBLICAL GUIDELINES

1. Bible Reading: Esther 6

2. Bible Reference: Exodus 17:14

> ***"And the LORD said unto Moses, write this for a memorial in a book and rehearse it in the ear of Joshua: for I will utterly put out the remembrance of Amalek from under heaven"***

3. Positive Confession: Hebrew 4:12

"For the word of God is quick, and powerful, and sharper than any two edged sword, piercing even to the dividing asunder of soul and spirit, and of the joints and marrow, and is a discerner of the thoughts and intents of the heart"

4. Champion prayer: My name shall be found in the book of life, in the name of Jesus.

5. Fasting: 6am-6pm.

6. Time of prayer: 12pm – 3am.

7. Duration of prayer: 7 days fasting and prayer.

PRAYER POINTS

1. Every danger that lurk around me scatter, in the name of Jesus

2. Slave dragons that want to turn me to slave in the dream die, in the name of Jesus

3. Trouble shooters that abuse my right in the dream, die in the name of Jesus

4. Monitoring powers assign to monitor me, die in the name of Jesus

5. Powers that want to kill spirit of evangelism in me, die in the name of Jesus

6. Every danger ahead of me scatter, in the name of Jesus

7. Powers that oppress me in the dream, die, in the name of Jesus

8. Powers assign to pull down my ministry, die in the name of Jesus

9. Thou evil master in charge of my case, die in the name of Jesus

10. Evil instrument assign against me, break to pieces, in the name of Jesus

11. Strongman in charge of my situation die, in the name of Jesus

12. Arrow of forgetfulness fired against me backfire in the name of Jesus

13. Arrows fired against me in my youth, come out and die in the name of Jesus

14. Arrow of setback fired against me, backfire in the name of Jesus

15. Evil arrow fired against my career backfire, in the name of Jesus

16. Anti-evangelism arrow fired against me backfire, in the name of Jesus

17. Arrow of sadness fired against my life, backfire in the name of Jesus

18. Arrow of insanity fired against my head, backfire in the name of Jesus

19. Rivers of problem flowing into my life, dry up in the name of Jesus

20. Thou cup of problem I shall not drink from you, in the name of Jesus

21. Spirit of evangelism in my life, receive fire and blossom in the name of Jesus

22. O Lord, give me sound mind to do research in your work.

23. Ministerial agony pack your load and leave my career, in the name of Jesus

24. Marital agony pack your load and leave my home in the name of Jesus

25. Arrow of darkness fired against the gathering of the saints, backfire

26. My destiny, refuse evil command, in the name of Jesus

27. I shall not be a prisoner of Satan, in the name of Jesus

28. O Lord, give me power to draw my sheep, closer and nearer to you

29. O Lord, give me understanding of the Word, in the name of Jesus

30. O Lord, let my prayer receive answer from your divine throne, in the name of Jesus

31. Powers assign to scatter my prayer, die, in the name of Jesus

32. My prayer, go deep to my problem and solve it, in the name of Jesus

33. O Lord, make me shepherd with zeal for God in the name of Jesus

34. My eyes, receive divine touch of God, in the name of Jesus

35. Every embargo placed upon my destiny scatter, in the name of Jesus

36. Embargo of "Thou shall not excel", placed upon my life, scatter in the name of Jesus

37. I shall not occupy dark seat of valley, in the name of Jesus

38. Every dark property in my possession, catch fire, and roast to ashes

39. I fumigate my bookshelf in the spirit with blood of Jesus to kill and destroy, evils in it

40. Satanic exchange in my bookshelf, stop in the name of Jesus

41. I replace every book of life exchanged with evil deposit in the bookshelf of God in my home

42. I fire back arrow of prayerlessness fired against me, in the name of Jesus

43. I hold broom of deliverance, and cleanse my spiritual cupboard in the name of Jesus

44. O Lord, I surrender my life to you for ever and ever

45. O Lord, Jesus Christ of Nazareth, show me your love

46. O Lord, Jesus Christ of Nazareth, fulfill your promise upon me

47. Good doors of God open to my life, in the name of Jesus

48. Thou doors of darkness assign for me, catch fire and roast to ashes

49. Every wickedness of the wicked against me scatter in the name of Jesus

50. I shall not bow or obey evil command in the name of Jesus

51. Blood of Jesus, cover my destiny, in the name of Jesus

52. Blood of Jesus, cover my property, in the name of Jesus

53. Blood of Jesus, cover my career, in the name of Jesus

54. O Lord, forgive me of sins Satan may use as legal ground to accuse me, in the name of Jesus

55. Sins that invite problem to life, quit me, as I quit you, in the name of Jesus

56. O Lord, make me a gallant preacher of the Word, in the name of Jesus

57. O Lord, make me a soldier of Christ, in the name of Jesus

58. My race shall not be in vain, in the name of Jesus

59. Holy Ghost Power, hold me to the end, in the name of Jesus

60. Angels of God, guide me 24 hours every day in the name of Jesus

61. Demons that invite problem to life, I silence you in the name of Jesus

62. Holy Spirit Divine put an end to problems in my life

63. My blessings appear by fire, in the name of Jesus

64. Every idol spirit in charge of my calling, I silence you in the name of Jesus

65. Oppression of Satan shall not rise second time in my life

66. My daily commitment is for God and mankind in the name of Jesus

67. Network of Satan for my life, scatter in the name of Jesus

68. I shall rise and not fall in the name of Jesus

CHAPTER 3

IF YOU SPLIT FIREWOOD IN THE DREAM

Satanic powers are officers in the temple of darkness marching about as commandos and merchants of destruction. They are villain, faceless, wicked and uncompromising. They are wicked militants that murder promising destiny and make good career unattractive.

To dream of splitting firewood in the dream is bad. It is like traveling on rough road of life. It is a dream that makes soul and destiny orphan. It is a dream war you must face with stamina and commitment. To split firewood in the dream without reward for it, suggests you are a servant in the spirit. It also suggests you shall labour heavily before you will feed. No matter your labour, it may not be fruitful, as a slave master in the spirit collects the reward in the spirit.

Once a life is under a slave master in the spirit, hatred, ill-luck, poverty and confusion may be the order of the day for him in real life. The reason is, since he works and serves a slave master in the spirit, he becomes useless to real employer or helpers in real life. You can't serve two masters at a time. Your efforts and dedication here is that of a slave to a slave master in the spirit. In real life, you may be hated or rejected by helpers or employer.

Thus, you are hooked to slavery in the spirit and need a way out.

THE WAY OUT

1. Pray and release yourself from slave master in the spirit
2. Break every stronghold that place you in captivity
3. Break covenant that exist between you and strange powers
4. Apply aggressive clinical investigative prayer that will expose spiritual criminals in the corridor of your life.
5. Reject, scatter and destroy criminal burden in your life
6. Cleanse yourself of evil marks that attract dark powers to life
7. Break every covenant with poverty
8. Drink blood of Jesus, to flush poverty in your blood stream.
9. Save your life from being a sinking ship. Pray against evil powers that make life unattractive to people.

10. Embrace hard work that brings result. Measure your input to work, and the harvest you reap.

11. Go for counsel before men of God that will give you good counsel on how to defeat the present situation you find yourself.

12. Go for deliverance in a living church that will pray you out of captivity.

13. Read good Christian prayer books. You can go for Fire for Fire prayer book to address this type of situation.

14. Let your Bible be your companion. Read and search for verses in the Bible you can apply to this type of situation.

15. Be a prayer warrior and a prayer warlord that make prayer a daily food.

16. Belief in dreams, don't sweep them under the carpet.

BIBLICAL GUIDELINE

1. Bible Reading: Exodus 5

2. Bible Reference: Lamentations 5:10

   "Our skin was block like an oven because of the terrible famine"

3. Positive Confession: Exodus 14:13

   "And Moses said unto the people, fear ye not, standstill, and see the salvation of the

LORD, which he will show to you today: for the Egyptians whom ye have seen today, ye shall see them again no more forever".

4. Champion Prayer: To God be the glory, the spirit of slavery in me is dead, in the name of Jesus.
5. Fasting: 6am – 6pm
6. Time of Prayer: 12pm – 3am
7. Duration of prayer: 14days fasting and prayer.

PRAYER POINTS

1. O Lord, disgrace every power assign to disgrace me, in the name of Jesus.
2. Powers that decide I will not make it in life die in the name of Jesus.
3. Every wall that stands between me and my breakthrough, I pull you down in the name of Jesus.
4. Slave master that acts as reward collector, making me to suffer, die in the name of Jesus.
5. Every embargo placed upon my breakthrough break in the name of Jesus.
6. Powers that vow I will labour and die, you are not my God die in the name of Jesus.
7. Every tool I use in the spirit to split firewood, I gather you and set it ablaze, therefore catch fire and roast to ashes in the name of Jesus.

8. Every rough road assign for me in the spirit, be converted to way of God for me.
9. Powers that turn me to servant in the dream die in the name of Jesus.
10. Wicked plans of the enemy to make my labour heavy without result scatter in the name of Jesus.
11. Arrow of hatred fired against me backfire and consume your sender in the name of Jesus.
12. Arrow of ill-luck fired against me backfire to your sender in the name of Jesus.
13. Arrow of poverty fired against me backfire in the name of Jesus.
14. Arrow of confusion fired against my life backfire in the name of Jesus.
15. Arrow of sickness and diseases fired against my life backfire in the name of Jesus.
16. Arrow of disgrace fired against me backfire in the name of Jesus.
17. Owner of evil load, carry your load in the name of Jesus.
18. Spiritual slavery affecting my career die in the name of Jesus.
19. Slave master chasing my helpers away die in the name of Jesus.
20. Temple of darkness in charge of my case, catch fire and roast to ashes in the name of Jesus.
21. Arrow of rejection fired against me backfire in the name of Jesus.

22. Any power or personality, that behaves like friend but attacking me in the spirit you are a failure in the name of Jesus.
23. Evil padlock fashion against me, break open in the name of Jesus.
24. Every covenant of failure I sign in the spirit break in the name of Jesus.
25. Every covenant of untimely death break, in the name of Jesus.
26. Every covenant of poverty assign to ruin my life break in the name of Jesus.
27. Every covenant of slavery I unconsciously enter, break in the name of Jesus.
28. Merchants of destruction monitoring me about die in the name of Jesus.
29. Every covenant that arise between me and strange powers break in the name of Jesus.
30. Spiritual criminals in charge of my case die in the name of Jesus.
31. Powers of darkness monitoring me about die in the name of Jesus.
32. Every criminal record enemy open for me, catch fire and roast to ashes in the name of Jesus.
33. Evil supervisors in charge of my life in the dream die in the name of Jesus.
34. You demon with faceless spirit die, in the name of Jesus.

35. Boastful Goliath threatening my existence, die in the name of Jesus.
36. Every wickedness of the wicked against my destiny die in the name of Jesus.
37. Every strongman of my father's house that turns me to slave in the spirit, your time is up die in the name of Jesus.
38. Every chain of darkness in my legs break to pieces in the name of Jesus.
39. Every chain of darkness in my hands break in the name of Jesus.
40. Every dark decision taken against me in the spirit, be nullified in the name of Jesus.
41. Any power assign to sink my destiny die in the name of Jesus.
42. O Lord, deliver me from powers that vow I will not make it in life.
43. Garment of slavery in my body, I pull you off and set you ablaze in the name of Jesus.
44. My career shall not scatter in the name of Jesus.
45. Slave master in charge of my life in the spirit die in the name of Jesus.
46. I break every stronghold of darkness holding me captive, in the name of Jesus.
47. Evil marks in my body, I cleanse you with blood of Jesus.
48. Evil marks that chase helpers away, I rebuke you, expire in the name of Jesus.

49. Evil marks in my body be converted to mark of God that attracts goodness to life.
50. Any power that says I will die as slave in the spirit, die in the name of Jesus.
51. O Lord, crown me with crown of breakthrough in the name of Jesus.
52. O Lord, bless every work I do with success in the name of Jesus.
53. My labour in the spirit be converted to financial bonus in real life in the name of Jesus.
54. My spirit in the valley of life, escape and locate me for signs and wonders.
55. What I lost in the spirit to slave masters, I recover you by fire in the name of Jesus.
56. Angels of God, come to my help, set me free from spirit slave master.
57. I refuse to carry out evil order in the dream in the name of Jesus.
58. I drink blood of Jesus, to uproot evil plantation in my body.
59. I drink blood of Jesus to flush evil plantation in my body.
60. I drink blood of Jesus to energize me against powers of darkness.
61. O Lord, save me from the hands of evil power that vow I will be his slave.
62. Thou works of my hand bring breakthrough in the name of Jesus.

63. My destiny shall not sink in the ocean of waste in the name of Jesus.
64. My heavenly anointed counsellors locate me in the name of Jesus.
65. O Lord, let my cup of joy full and runneth over in the name of Jesus.
66. I shall be the head and not the tail in the name of Jesus.

CHAPTER 4

IF YOU SEE HOLE IN YOUR POCKET OR PURSE IN THE DREAM

Financial drainers are everywhere looking for pockets to drain. They look smart and friendly but are loaded with evil intention. They trick and bring victims to financial zero level. They punch holes in the pockets and bank accounts until it leaned.

Hole in the pocket is witchcraft driven. It foretells upcoming attack against your finance, business, or career. It is a dream to watch and examine because it adds no value to life. Holes in the pocket foretell you will spend on what you don't need, or on what may not yield income. Many fall victim by their attitude or when under demonic influence. They are cornered by Satan who drain and reduce them to penury. A leaking pocket makes saving difficult. It is loaded with extravagant and reckless spending. As victim spends lavishly, Satan makes them feel high and cool. This is the trick of Satan.

The summary of seeing holes in the pocket in the dream are spirit of reckless spending, leaking pocket, arrow of poverty, unaccountable expenses, non-payment of tithe etc. Today many lives are in the valley of debt; unable to liberate themselves from poverty. They incur debt because they live ostentatious life style and spend lavishly on alcohol, drugs, parties, women, clothes and other things that add no value to life. They lend without control with attitude of good Samaritan that ruin life.

THE WAY OUT

1. If you lend people money, ensure it have control and limit. Collect debts out there first, before embarking on another good Samaritan adventure.
2. Pray against looters in the spirit that loot men in the dream only to wake into lean purse of bankruptcy.
3. Drop bad habit that impair progress. Habit is a shirt made of iron. The best way to break a bad habit is to drop it.
4. Don't suck into pledge you can't redeem. Avoid sitting on "high tables" that will make you pledge what you can't fulfill. To shamefully fulfill ambiguous pledge cause holes in the pocket.

5. Avoid making bad situation worse by investing on what drains the pocket. It may damage your image and create credibility problem

6. Abstain from worldly behaviour that drains pocket; such as consumption of alcohol, cigarette smoking, drug addiction, lust, purchase of worldly clothes and materials.

7. Control your anger, it kills, makes you blind, foolish that leads to court action that drain pocket. When Cain's heart was filled with anger, murder was close by.

8. When you dream, take it serious; don't sweep it under the carpet. Know the meaning and take right step

9. In this situation be a prayer warrior and a prayer warlord

10. Read the Word. Let your Holy Bible be your companion. Read it and meditate on it day and night

11. Read good Christian books that improves spiritually and physically

12. Surrender your life to Jesus and quit sin

BIBLE GUIDELINE

1. Bible Reading: Luke 15

2. Bible Reference: Haggai 1:6

> *"Ye have sown much, and bring in little, ye eat, but ye have not enough, ye drink, but ye are not filled with drink: ye clothe you, but there is none warm; and he that earneth wages earneth wages to put it into a bag with holes"*

3. Positive confession: Mathew 13:213

> *"But he that received seed into the good ground is he that heareth the word, and understandeth it, which also beareth fruit, and bringeth forth, some an hundred fold, some sixty, some thirty*

4. Champion prayer: The fruit of my labour shall not disappear to the wind, in the name of Jesus. Amen

5. Fasting: 6am- 6pm

6. Time of Prayer: 12pm – 3am

7. Duration of prayer: 9 days fasting and prayer

PRAYER POINT

1. Any power that sits on my harvest summersault and die, in the name of Jesus

2. O Lord, forgive me of sins that brought me to this position, in the name of Jesus

3. O Lord, make me triumph over every accusation to nail me financially, in the name of Jesus

4. O Lord, make me wise to understand my environment in the name of Jesus

5. Financial drainers in my life, die in the name of Jesus

6. Powers that want to make my harvest heap of ruins, die in the name of Jesus

7. Powers that make helpers flee from me, die in the name of Jesus

8. Powers that want to waste me like desert no one visits die, in the name of Jesus

9. Any power assign to scatter my finance, die, in the name of Jesus

10. Financial drainers in my in-law's house, assign to drain my purse die in the name of Jesus

11. Desert spirit in my life, die in the name of Jesus

12. People that deceived me, and bring me low, be exposed and be disgraced, in the name of Jesus

13. Any power that wants me to eat bitter food, die in the name of Jesus

14. Any power that wants me to drink poisoned water die, in the name of Jesus

15. People that run to me for help, shall not eventually feed me again in the name of Jesus

16. Financial drainers in my father's house draining my finance die in the name of Jesus

17. Financial drainers in my mother's house draining my finance die in the name of Jesus

18. Financial drainers in my place of work, die in the name of Jesus

19. Blood of Jesus, cleanse sign of poverty written on my forehead, in the name of Jesus

20. Rituals of the past fighting me back, die in the name of Jesus

21. Prodigal spirit in me, die in the name of Jesus

22. Spirit that discourage me from saving die in the name of Jesus

23. Arrow of poverty fired against my life, backfire, in the name of Jesus

24. Arrow of failure, fired against my life, backfire in the name of Jesus

25. Spirit that makes me lend without control die in the name of Jesus

26. Looters in the spirit in my life die, in the name of Jesus

27. Anger that drain pocket, expire, in the name of Jesus

28. Attitude that drain pocket leave me alone and die in the name of Jesus

29. I shall not invest on vain ventures in the name of Jesus

30. Bad habit that impair progress in my life die, in the name of Jesus
31. Pledges of financial shame die in the name of Jesus
32. I shall not swim in the ocean of failure in the name of Jesus
33. I shall not go bankrupt in the name of Jesus
34. O Lord, reverse my loss to gain in the name of Jesus
35. O Lord, reverse my sorrow to joy in the name of Jesus
36. O Lord, reverse my financial mourn to financial harvest in the name of Jesus
37. O Lord, reverse my debit to credit in the name of Jesus
38. My eyes, become fountain of joy in the name of Jesus
39. O Lord, fill me with power to repent in the name of Jesus
40. Holes in my pocket, expire, in the name of Jesus
41. Adventures that leak pocket expire, in the name of Jesus
42. Bad managers in the spirit, shall not manage my finance, in the name of Jesus
43. I shall not beg before I feed in the name of Jesus

44. Financial shame, quit my life in the name of Jesus

45. My wounds, be healed in the name of Jesus

46. O Lord, silence my enemy in the name of Jesus

47. Thou dark power, vomit my treasure in your stomach in the name of Jesus

48. I silence power of poverty in my life, in the name of Jesus

49. Every pot cooking my success, break in the name of Jesus

50. Instrument of darkness against my success, break to pieces in the name of Jesus

51. Blood of Jesus, seal every hole in my pocket, in the name of Jesus

52. Blood of Jesus cover me from head to my toes, in the name of Jesus

53. My pursue, receive divine touch in the name of Jesus

54. My bank account, receive divine touch in the name of Jesus

55. I shall not sow much and reap little in the name of Jesus

56. Poverty shall not reign in my life, in the name of Jesus

57. I shall not earn wages to put it into a bag of holes, in the name of Jesus

58. Bountiful harvest, be my portion in the name of Jesus

59. I recover all I lost in the dream and in the physical in the name of Jesus

60. I will be among, who is who, in my country, in the name of Jesus

61. I shall celebrate over my enemy in the name of Jesus

62. What I gather, enemy will not scatter it in the name of Jesus

63. My pursue shall grow and meet my needs in the name of Jesus

64. Financial drainers, hand off my life in the name of Jesus

65. Time of financial error is over in my life in the name of Jesus

66. I will enjoy long life, wealth and honour in the name of Jesus

CHAPTER 5

IF YOU PLANT IN THE DESERT IN THE DREAM

Desert in the spirit portends an upcoming hopeless situation that may lead to loneliness, famine and hardship. It signifies arrow of poverty, want and isolation.

It is therefore sign of sorrow in the offing, if you plant in the desert in the dream. This is a situation you don't find water to wet your plants or have rain fall. What this mean is that helpers may not be found when the need arises, or you may experience close heaven.

If you don't apply acidic prayer to nullify such dream, it may lead to chain of problems. As a result, your career, ministry and finance may be affected with multiple satanic bombardments. If you are engulfed in it, your children may suffer what they shouldn't.

What a mess caused by inability to interpret dream and cancel it with right prayer? Thus, you may end up in poverty, anger, sickness and what have you. It is time you nullify effects of bad dreams.

Enough is enough, you shall not labour in vain. Amen.

THE WAY OUT

1. Believe that dream has meaning. You don't dream for dream sake, there is message about to be passed to you. Have meaning to your dream and take action.

2. Be a prayer warrior and be persistent in it. Human life is full of ups and down. There has never been a time we sing a song of total deliverance and freedom from dark powers that kill destinies of men.

3. Call upon the Lord for divine wisdom to build robust risk management system that tackle issues as they arise.

4. Fire back evil arrows enemy fire against you. You are a candidate of success, not failure.

5. Re-engineer your attitude and habit to magnetise good and responsible people to you, so that helpers may locate you.

6. Pray to God for land that flow with milk and honey instead of desert

7. Cover yourself, your seeds (career), your crop (expectation and results) with blood of Jesus. Your labour must not be in vain.

8. Go for deliverance in a reputable church.

9. Read the Word and apply verses and chapters in the Bible that correlate with situations as they arise

10. Read Christian living books. Lay hands on my books titled Fire for Fire, Dictionary of dreams, Prayer to Locate Helpers etc., and pull down your Goliath.

11. Above all, be a born again Christian so that you may be on the Lord's side all the time.

12. Seek the face of God anytime you want to set up your ministry. It is dangerous to set up a ministry in wrong location.

BIBLICAL GUIDELINE

1. Bible Reading: Judges 6

2. Bible Reference: Mathew 3:3

> ***"For this is he that was spoken of by the prophet Esaias, saying, the voice of one crying in the wilderness, prepare ye the way of the Lord, make his paths straight"***

3. Positive Confession: Isaiah 54:10

> ***"For the mountains shall depart and the hills he removed, but my kindness shall not depart from thee, neither shall the***

covenant of my peace be removed, saith the LORD that hath mercy on thee"

4. Champion Prayer: Heavenly success, locate me by fire in the name of Jesus.
5. Fasting: 6am – 6pm
6. Time of Prayer: 12pm – 3am
7. Duration of prayer: 7days fasting and prayer.

PRAYER POINTS

1. O Lord, rebuke desert spirit assign to trouble me in the name of Jesus.
2. Every desert spirit assign to monitor me, die in the name of Jesus.
3. Dark Spirit assign to make me set up business in a wrong place, die in the name of Jesus.
4. Powers assign to ensure I establish my ministry where it will fail, die in the name of Jesus.
5. Powers assign to direct my step to wrong place, die in the name of Jesus.
6. Desert spirit in my father's house, die in the name of Jesus.
7. Desert spirit in my mother's house, die in the name of Jesus.
8. Desert spirit in my in-law's house assign to pull me down, die in the name of Jesus.

9. Powers assign to kill my helpers; what do you think you are doing? die in the name of Jesus.

10. Power of famine, leave me alone and die in the name of Jesus.

11. Powers assign to build wall of hardship around me, die in the name of Jesus.

12. Powers assign to sink my life, die in the name of Jesus.

13. Chain of problems in readiness to consume me, break in the name of Jesus.

14. Evil soil allotted to me in the spirit, disappear in the name of Jesus.

15. Every effort of enemy to let me embark on wasted journey, come to an end today in the name of Jesus.

16. Powers behind close heaven against me, your time is up, die in the name of Jesus.

17. Satanic bombardment against me, stop by fire in the name of Jesus.

18. Power that pursue my parents, and is now after me, you made a mistake, therefore die

19. Poverty that trouble my father, and now troubling me, die in the name of Jesus.

20. Poverty that trouble my mother, and now troubling me, die in the name of Jesus.

21. Poverty that trouble my in-laws and now after my household, die in the name of Jesus.

22. Arrow of hardship fired against my life, backfire in the name of Jesus.
23. Arrow of poverty fired against me; backfire in the name of Jesus.
24. Arrow of disgrace fired against me; backfire in the name of Jesus.
25. Arrow of famine fired against me; backfire in the name of Jesus.
26. Arrow of loneliness fired against me; backfire in the name of Jesus.
27. Spirit of anger assign to divert my glory to shame, shall fail in the name of Jesus.
28. Evil warehouse with my wealth, release it by fire in the name of Jesus.
29. Garment of shame in my body, I pull you off, catch fire and roast to ashes in the name of Jesus.
30. Sickness assign to sap me dry, die in the name of Jesus.
31. Evil messenger assign to give me sad news, my life is not available, die on your way in the name of Jesus.
32. Every covenant with poverty in my life, break in the name of Jesus.
33. Every covenant with sickness in my life, break in the name of Jesus.

34. Every covenant with failure in my life, break in the name of Jesus.

35. Forces assign against my destiny, die in the name of Jesus.

36. Wicked activities of enemies against my life scatter in the name of Jesus.

37. Powers monitoring my breakthrough in the spirit, die in the name of Jesus.

38. Curses pronounced against my parents that is now after me, backfire in the name of Jesus.

39. Curses pronounced against my breakthrough, break in the name of Jesus.

40. Spirit of almost there troubling my destiny, die in the name of Jesus.

41. Weapons of darkness, work against my enemies in the name of Jesus.

42. Instrument of darkness assign to bury my destiny, catch fire and roast to ashes

43. Spirit of un-seriousness in my life, die in the name of Jesus.

44. Breakthrough aborts in my life, die in the name of Jesus.

45. Difficult times in my life, expire in the name of Jesus.

46. I cover myself with blood of Jesus

47. I cover my investment with blood of Jesus

48. I cover my finance with blood of Jesus

49. Satan, turn back from pursuing me with your weapon in the name of Jesus.
50. My Father, my father, start good thing in my life, in the name of Jesus.
51. I apply honey to the garden of my life in the name of Jesus.
52. Oh heaven, open and bless me in the name of Jesus.
53. Heavenly rain, wet and nourish the plant of my life in the name of Jesus.
54. My ministry, hear the word of the Lord, receive divine anointing in the name of Jesus.
55. Thou seed of my ministry, germinate and blossom in the name of Jesus.
56. Thou seed of my business germinate and blossom in the name of Jesus.
57. Desert in my life, disappear in the name of Jesus.
58. Long-time rain that refuse to fall, what are you waiting for, let there be rain, fall by fire in the name of Jesus.
59. Helpers appear in my situation in the name of Jesus.
60. Helpers in the corridor of my life, wake up and help me in the name of Jesus.
61. I will not labour in vain in the name of Jesus.

62. I shall overcome every up and down, I face in life in the name of Jesus.

63. O Lord, give me wisdom that kills poverty in the name of Jesus.

64. I remain candidate of success not failure in the name of Jesus.

65. My character, magnetize success to my life in the name of Jesus.

66. O Lord, settle me in the land that flow with milk and honey in the name of Jesus.

67. O Lord, direct my step rightly and timely to achieve my goals in the name of Jesus.

68. O Lord, let your kindness and favour be my portion forever and ever. Amen.

CHAPTER 6

IF ARRAIGNED IN THE COURT OF DARKNESS IN THE DREAM

Court of darkness is a witchcraft court organized and overseen by wicked powers. It is a place where negative judgement is posed on victims. Nothing good comes out it.

It is therefore dangerous to be arraigned in a wicked and dark court of this nature. Court of darkness portends a place of woe and calamity where destiny is truncated, where destiny is abused, where destiny is caged and destroyed. Thus, to be prosecuted in a dark court is writing letter to disaster.

Joy or laughter hardly takes place in court of darkness. It is always sadness and cry. Innocent souls perish unnoticed. While many are jailed in dark courts, many are either chained to a spot, hand cuffed or tied to a spot.

It is a court house occupied by faceless judge and heartless prosecutors; evil accusers, dark police officers and mindless soldiers. They collaborate to kill and to destroy destiny. Agony and cry is there trade mark. This is the type of court enemy may arraign you in the dream.

It is therefore a must to pray and set yourself free from evil of darkness.

THE WAY OUT

1. Don't play with your dream, belief it and find right interpretation to it. God wants to send you message, so that you might take right step in the right direction.
2. Pray and break every shackle, evil handcuff and chains enemy may envelope your destiny with.
3. Call upon God to send thunder and fire to consume evil court house arranged for you
4. Pray for fire of Holy Ghost to surround you and ward off dark powers that may molest or arrest you in the dream.
5. Overturn wicked judgement of the enemy. Appeal your case to God and counter very wicked judgement passed against you. Let Jesus be your Senior Advocate.
6. Break every covenant that may exist between you and dark powers.
7. Pray without ceasing, so that you may not be victim of evil arrester.

8. Break every yoke that may render you useless or make you a failure in life.

9. Tear to pieces evil garment or prison uniform enemy assign for you in the spirit.

10. Go for deliverance in a living church.

11. Read the Word, your Bible is a treasure book of deliverance, protection, warfare, love, sanctification, knowledge of God etc.

12. Read good Christian books that improve life.

13. Seek God's favour, mercy and protection to scatter rules and order of dark powers.

BIBLICAL GUIDELINE

1. Bible Reading: Acts of Apostle 25

2. Bible Reference: Daniel 3:13

   "Then Nebuchadnezzar in his rage and fury commanded to bring Shadrach, Meshach and Abednego. Then they brought those men before the King".

3. Positive Confession: Isaiah 8:9-10.

   9 ***"Associate yourselves, O ye people, and ye shall be broken in piecies, and give ear, all ye of far countries: gird yourselves, and ye shall be broken in pieces, gird yourselves, and ye shall be broken in pieces.***

> **10 *Take counsel together and it shall come to nought, speak the word, and it shall not stand for God is with us"***

4. Champion prayer: Court of darkness assign to judge me catch fire and roast to ashes, in the name of Jesus. Amen.
5. Fasting: 6am – 6pm
6. Time of prayer: 12pm – 3am
7. Duration of prayer: 7days fasting and prayer.

PRAYER POINTS

1. O Lord, stop activities of courts of darkness against me in the name of Jesus.
2. Lord Jesus, let your blood flow in court of darkness and scatter them
3. Lord Jesus, place your cross in court of darkness and scatter it
4. Lord Jesus, let your blood flow on the seat of evil judge in charge of my case, and unseat him
5. Lord Jesus, lay your cross on seat of evil judge and unseat him
6. O Lord, confuse the language of powers against me in the court of darkness in the name of Jesus.
7. Fire of God, burn to ashes evil register that has myname in the name of Jesus.

8. Witchcraft court organized to sentence me to jail, catch fire and roast to ashes in the name of Jesus.
9. Witchcraft court organized to sentence me to death, catch fire and roast to ashes in the name of Jesus.
10. Witchcraft court organized to put me to shame, catch fire and toast to ashes in the name of Jesus.
11. Witchcraft court organized to naked me financially, catch fire and roast to ashes in the name of Jesus.
12. Witchcraft court, catch fire and roast with your documents in the name of Jesus.
13. Every woe and calamity that emanate in the court of darkness against me, scatter in the name of Jesus.
14. Every court of darkness assign against my destiny, scatter in the name of Jesus.
15. My destiny, arise over dark abuse in the name of Jesus.
16. My destiny be released from evil cage, in the name of Jesus.
17. Prosecutors against me in the dream, die in the name of Jesus.
18. I reverse wicked judgement passed against me in the dream in the name of Jesus.

19. Yoke of evil judgement upon my life, break in the name of Jesus.
20. Handcuff of darkness in my hands, break in the name of Jesus.
21. Every rope used to tie me down to one spot, break to piece and catch fire in the name of Jesus.
22. Thou dark police assign to arrest me in the dream, die on your way in the name of Jesus.
23. Dark judge on seat to judge me, summersault and die in the name of Jesus.
24. Accusers of my soul, die in the name of Jesus.
25. Thunder of God, strike and kill accusers assign to testify against me in the name of Jesus.
26. Court house of darkness assign against me, catch fire and roast to ashes,
27. Fathers and shackles in my leg, break in the name of Jesus.
28. Holy Ghost fire, surround me and ward off enemies around me in the name of Jesus.
29. Every covenant between me and dark power, break in the name of Jesus.
30. Cup of sorrow awaiting me, break in the name of Jesus.
31. Arrow of sadness, fired against me in the court of darkness, backfire in the name of Jesus.

32. Arrow of nakedness, fired against me in the court of darkness, backfire in the name of Jesus.

33. Arrows of failure, fired against me in the court of darkness, backfire in the name of Jesus.

34. Arrow of defeat, fired against me in the court of darkness, backfire in the name of Jesus.

35. Soldiers assign to arrest me in the dream, die in the name of Jesus.

36. Soldiers assign to guide me in captivity, sleep and die in the name of Jesus.

37. Evil garment that drag me into problem, catch fire and roast to ashes in the name of Jesus.

38. Prison uniform prepared for me in the spirit, catch fire and roast to ashes in the name of Jesus.

39. O Lord, break the head of the wicked with rod in the name of Jesus.

40. Powers assign to take me to jail, die in the name of Jesus.

41. Powers assign to turn my joy to sorrow, die in the name of Jesus.

42. Powers assign to turn my harvest to famine, die in the name of Jesus.

43. Opportunity wasters in my life, die in the name of Jesus.

44. Powers assign to re-arrange my destiny to failure, die in the name of Jesus.

45. Destiny arrester, hear the word of the Lord, I am not your candidate; die in the name of Jesus.

46. Testimony arrester, hear the word of the Lord, I am not your candidate; die in the name of Jesus.

47. Holy Ghost Power, counter every judgement of darkness passed against me in the name of Jesus.

48. Lord Jesus, be my Advocate and nullify evil judgement of Satan in the name of Jesus.

49. I am loaded with grace of God in the name of Jesus.

50. I am loaded with favour of God in the name of Jesus.

51. I ride in horse of God out of court of darkness in the name of Jesus.

52. The battle changed, I handcuff my enemy to the court of God in the name of Jesus.

53. My soul, escape from captivity of Satan in the name of Jesus.

54. Lord Jesus, overturn every judgement against me in the name of Jesus.

55. I will not dwell in prison yard in the name of Jesus.

56. God of war, release me from evil soldiers, in the name of Jesus.

57. God of war, release me from police of darkness in the name of Jesus.

58. I will not perish in the journey of life in the name of Jesus.
59. O Lord, fill my heart with laughter and joy in the name of Jesus.
60. Power to pray and receive answer fall upon me in the name of Jesus.
61. O Lord, deliver me and let me possess my possession in the name of Jesus.
62. My destiny, reject dark judgement in the name of Jesus.
63. Failure shall not slaughter my hope, in the name of Jesus.
64. Accusers of my life shall fail woefully in the name of Jesus.
65. Prison yard victims, is minus me and my family, in the name of Jesus.
66. My God shall command success unto me in the name of Jesus.
67. My destiny is loaded with miracles in the name of Jesus.
68. Thank you O Lord, as I laugh over my enemies in the name of Jesus. Amen.

CHAPTER 7

IF YOU EXPERIENCE SNAKE BITE IN THE DREAM

Snake bite in the dream is a dangerous attack in the spirit. Snakes are controlled by serpentine spirit. It is a deceptive and cruel spirit with the aim to kill and cause untimely death. Snake bite in the dream is a forerunner of sudden death, health hazard and poverty.

Snake bite in the dream connotes you are dealing with friends of questionable character, people of double standard and treacherous persons. Snakes, either small or big, are dangerous. Snakes are named; rattlesnake, python, boa, viper, cobra, mamba etc. Whatever name snake bears, it is dangerous.

You can't live in a room with snake, unless you worship it as god, or you send it on errand for evil mission. Thus, snakes can be sent to attack or kill in the spirit. It is therefore proper, to pray for strength to kill any evil snake sent from the pit of hell to attack you.

In general, snake has spiritual meaning of deception, danger, hatred, evil, threat, witchcraft attack, troubles, obstacle and treachery. A dream of snake bite portends a period of struggle against evil attack.

Snake bite is not what should be treated lightly. It is good to equip yourself in prayer before you are attacked or harmed by wicked powers.

THE WAY OUT

1. The foundational way out, is to belief that dreams are real. When you dream of snake bite, don't take it lightly. Address it spiritually.
2. Cover yourself with blood of Jesus to serve as spiritual garment and immunity against evil bites.
3. Keep away from sin. Enemy may use it as yardstick to attack you in your sleep.
4. Return every evil arrow back to sender
5. Cancel and nullify effects of snake bite in the dream
6. Drink blood of Jesus to neutralize and purge you of snake bite poison in the dream
7. Pray that every serpentine power assign against you should die
8. Be a born again Christian and live in Christ

9. Be filled with Holy Spirit and power all the time
10. Do not go to bed in fear. Always invite Jesus and Holy Ghost power to guide you with their awesome power.
11. Pray without ceasing
12. Read and know the Word. Apply it appropriately to situations
13. Read living Christian books. Use Fire for Fire prayer book to fight this battle and Dictionary of Dreams to know more of dreams and their interpretations. This book has about ten thousand dreams and interpretations.

BIBLICAL GUIDELINE

1. Bible Reading: Act of Apostles 28
2. Bible Reference: Genesis 3:15

   "And I will put enmity between thee and the woman, and between thy seed and her seed, it shall bruise thy head, and thou shalt bruise his heel".

3. Positive Confession: Psalm 91:7

   "A thousand shall fall at thy side, and ten thousand at thy right hand; but it shall not come nigh thee".

4. Champion prayer: Every wickedness of the wicked against my life scatter in the name of Jesus.
5. Fasting: 6am – 6pm
6. Time for prayer: 12pm – 3am
7. Duration for prayer: 12days fasting and prayer.

PRAYER POINTS

1. Lord Jesus, empower me to match upon serpent and scorpion unhurt in the name of Jesus.
2. Lord Jesus, heal me of snake bite in the dream, in the name of Jesus.
3. Lord Jesus, laminate my body against snake bite in the name of Jesus.
4. I drink blood of Jesus, to kill poison of snake bite in the dream
5. I drink blood of Jesus, to purge evil deposit in my body in the name of Jesus.
6. Blood of Jesus, flow in my body against powers of darkness.
7. Serpentine spirit pursuing me in the dream, die in the name of Jesus.
8. Every cruel move of the enemy against me, backfire in the name of Jesus.
9. Every deception against me in the spirit, scatter in the name of Jesus.

10. Python assign against me, die in the name of Jesus.

11. Cobra assign against me, die in the name of Jesus.

12. Holy Spirit, inject every serpent assign against me to death in the name of Jesus.

13. Every flying serpent, be electrocuted in the name of Jesus.

14. Every crawling serpent, crawl to fire of God and burn to ashes in the name of Jesus.

15. Serpent on a spot, waiting to attack me, be strike down by thunder fire of God in the name of Jesus.

16. Let every evil tree that harbour serpent of darkness wither in the name of Jesus.

17. Let evil habitation of serpent assign against me, catch fire and roast to ashes in the name of Jesus.

18. Let the serpent that attack from the rock die in the name of Jesus.

19. Let the serpent that attack from waters die in the name of Jesus.

20. Let the serpent that attack from land die in the name of Jesus.

21. Let the serpent that attack from hiding places die in the name of Jesus.

22. I break the head of serpent assign to attack me in the name of Jesus.
23. I break the spinal cord of serpent assign to attack me, in the name of Jesus.
24. I cut the head of serpent assign against me in the name of Jesus.
25. Every arrow of sudden death fired against me in the dream; backfire in the name of Jesus.
26. Every arrow of sickness fired against me in the spirit; backfire in the name of Jesus.
27. Every arrow of sorrow fired against me in the spirit; backfire in the name of Jesus.
28. Every arrow of poverty fired against me in the spirit backfire in the name of Jesus.
29. Every arrow of backwardness fired against me in the spirit; backfire in the name of Jesus.
30. Friends of questionable character around me be exposed and be disgraced in the name of Jesus.
31. Unfriendly friends that gather in order to harm me be disgraced in the name of Jesus.
32. Serpent on errand of evil mission against me die, in the name of Jesus.
33. Serpent assign to attack me in the spirit, die in the name of Jesus.
34. Serpent assign to kill me in the spirit, die in the name of Jesus.

35. Any serpent sent from the pit of hell to attack me, die in the name of Jesus.

36. Every danger around me, scatter in the name of Jesus.

37. Danger of Satan, bow to power of God, in the name of Jesus.

38. Danger from the pit of hell, melt away in the name of Jesus.

39. Danger snaring at me, die in the name of Jesus.

40. Spirit of hatred injected into my life as a result of snake attack come out and die in the name of Jesus.

41. Troubles around me scatter in the name of Jesus.

42. Every obstacle that stand between me and success, scatter in the name of Jesus.

43. I laminate my life with blood of Jesus.

44. I drink blood of Jesus to neutralize and destroy poison of serpent in my life.

45. I drink blood of Jesus to purge me of evil deposit in the name of Jesus.

46. Every witchcraft attack against my destiny, scatter in the name of Jesus.

47. I cover myself with blood of Jesus to serve as immunity against snake bite

48. Lord Jesus, let your blood that cover me become garment that ward off evil in the name of Jesus.
49. Lord Jesus, forgive me of sins that open door to enemy in my life.
50. I fumigate my environment with blood of Jesus, against evil attack in the name of Jesus.
51. I cancel and nullify effect of snake in the dream in the name of Jesus.
52. Every viper that fasten itself on my hand, die in the name of Jesus.
53. Every viper that fasten itself on my leg, die in the name of Jesus.
54. I receive strength to kill serpent in the dream in the name of Jesus.
55. I shake serpent in my hand into fire of destruction in the name of Jesus.
56. I shake serpent in my leg into fire of destruction in the name of Jesus.
57. I shall suffer no effect from evil attack in the name of Jesus.
58. Holy Spirit of God, fill me and direct my step, in the name of Jesus.
59. Lord Jesus, I invite you be with me all the time
60. I receive divine healing in the name of Jesus.
61. By his stripe, I am healed in the name of Jesus.

62. I shall not die but live to praise the Lord, in the name of Jesus.

63. My promotion, appear by fire in the name of Jesus.

64. Favour of God, be my daily food in the name of Jesus.

65. Every grip of poverty in my life shall fail in the name of Jesus.

66. I step into coast of success and possess my possession in the name of Jesus.

67. My prayer, receive heavenly answer in the name of Jesus.

68. I shall testify to the glory of God in the name of Jesus.

69. I shall not be weak but strong in the name of Jesus.

CHAPTER 8

IF YOU ARE CURSED IN THE DREAM

A curse is evil pronouncement upon a life. It is a negative testament that erodes life. If pronounced upon a life and it manifests, it can make the cursed insane, poor, stagnant in life or die untimely death. It is therefore a tragedy, if a person is cursed in the dream.

The trade mark of curse in the dream includes among others, intimidation and fear in the heart. People that are cursed this way never make it in life. They either end up in the dust bin of life or waste away. Powers that curse people in the dream can best be describe as evil arresters, destiny killers, waster of life, arrow firers, demonic powers etc., whose mission is nothing but evil.

To be cursed in the dream is a mother of minus in a life. Multiple problems occur in such life, progress is retarded, stagnancy controls such destiny, poverty reigns, blockages set in, while impotence is pre-eminent. Dark power controls such life, enveloped in cloud of darkness.

It is therefore a must, to reverse and be set free of every manner of evil curse pronounced against you in the dream.

THE WAY OUT

1. Don't take this type of dream lightly. It is loaded with evil. Therefore, belief in dreams and ensure you interpret it well and address it.
2. Pray the prayer of back to sender. Pray that owner of evil load should carry his load.
3. Reverse every curse to blessing, success and breakthrough.
4. Let fire fall upon evil congregation assign against you
5. Pray that evil thought of the enemy to melt away.
6. Call on God to release you from darkroom of Satan
7. Live a righteous life so that God may have his protective eyes upon you. The righteous are in the save hands of God.
8. Don't visit false prophets that may turn around to curse you later in life.
9. Obey your parent; don't live to see their anger. Settle matters with them amicably. Even if they

are not in Christ, preach Christ to them with maturity.

10. Don't swear falsely so that the curse you pronounce does not come upon your head.

11. Go for deliverance, break and cancel evil curse pronounced against you.

12. Read the Bible and apply word of God upon your life

13. Cover yourself with blood of Jesus to immune you against evil curse.

14. Read living Christian books that will liberate you spiritually from wicked powers. Try your hands on my book Fire for Fire and Dictionary of Dreams.

BIBLICAL GUIDELINE

1. Bible Reading: 2 Samuel 16

2. Bible Reference: Genesis 27:12

   "My father peradventure will feel me, and I shall seam to him as a deceiver, and I shall bring a curse upon me, and not a blessing".

3. Positive Confession: Genesis 12:2-3

   2. . *"And I will make of thee a great nation, and I will bless thee, and make thy name great and thou shall be a blessing.*

3. ***And I will bless them that bless thee, and curse him that curseth thee: and in thee shall all families of the earth be blessed".***

4. Champion prayer: O Lord, break every curse fashion against me in the name of Jesus. Amen.

5. Fasting: 6am – 6pm

6. Time for prayer: 12pm – 3am

7. Duration for prayer: 14days fasting and prayer.

PRAYER POINTS

1. O Lord, curse them that curse me in the name of Jesus.

2. Every anti-favour deposit in my body, jump out and die in the name of Jesus.

3. Powers against my peace, die in the name of Jesus.

4. Hidden curse upon my life, break in the name of Jesus.

5. Parental curse upon my life, break in the name of Jesus.

6. Every wicked pronouncement against my life, backfire in the name of Jesus.

7. Fear, as a result of curse in the dream, expire in the name of Jesus.

8. Powers that curse me in the dream, die in the name of Jesus.

9. Evil arresters assign to arrest me in the dream, die in the name of Jesus.

10. Destiny killers assign to kill my destiny, die in the name of Jesus.

11. Powers that fire arrow against me be consumed with your arrow in the name of Jesus.

12. Demonic powers in charge of my situation, die in the name of Jesus.

13. Negative testament against my life, be reversed in the name of Jesus.

14. Multiple problems staring at me, scatter in the name of Jesus.

15. Cloud of darkness around me, disappear in the name of Jesus.

16. Destroying tongue, cliff to the roof of your mouth in the name of Jesus.

17. I cleanse every written curse against me with blood of Jesus

18. Every curse in the Bible, invade the home of my enemy, in the name of Jesus.

19. Every curse that says I shall not rise and shine, backfire in the name of Jesus.

20. Every curse that says, "I shall not let you go", you are a liar, backfire in the name of Jesus.

21. Every curse of bareness in my life, die in the name of Jesus.

22. Every curse of fear in my life backfire in the name of Jesus.
23. Hammer of God, break the head of powers cursing me in secret in the name of Jesus.
24. Load of darkness on my head, catch fire in the name of Jesus.
25. Every arrow of insanity fired against my life, backfire in the name of Jesus.
26. Every arrow of poverty fired against my life, backfire in the name of Jesus.
27. Every arrow of insanity fired against my life, backfire in the name of Jesus.
28. Every arrow of untimely death fired against my life, backfire in the name of Jesus.
29. Every arrow of stagnancy fired against my life, backfire in the name of Jesus.
30. Every tragedy aimed at me in the dream, die in the name of Jesus.\
31. O Lord, fill the life of people that curse me with emptiness in the name of Jesus.
32. Evil association against my life, scatter in the name of Jesus.
33. Fire of God, fall upon evil gathering targeted against me in the name of Jesus.
34. Every darkroom of darkness that hold me captive, expire in the name of Jesus.

35. Chain of darkness holding me captive, break in the name of Jesus.

36. Glory snatcher pursuing me about, die in the name of Jesus.

37. Witchdoctor monitoring me in the mirror, die in the name of Jesus.

38. Witchcraft darkroom, catch fire and roast to ashes in the name of Jesus.

39. Every false prophet on my way, clear away in the name of Jesus.

40. Wicked powers assign to scatter my destiny, die in the name of Jesus.

41. Every curse from neighbours, backfire in the name of Jesus.

42. Thou strongmen of my father's house waging war against me, die in the name of Jesus.

43. Blood of Jesus, flush evil deposit in my body caused by curse in the name of Jesus.

44. I immunize myself with blood of Jesus, against every curse in the name of Jesus.

45. Blood of Jesus, cleanse me of evil mark in my body

46. Owner of evil load, carry your load in the name of Jesus.

47. Announcement of rejection upon my life from kingdom of darkness, backfire in the name of Jesus.

48. Every curse pushing me back from getting to my promised land, scatter in the name of Jesus.

49. I reverse every curse of hardship to breakthrough in the name of Jesus.

50. I reverse every curse of trial and failure to multiple testimonies in the name of Jesus.

51. I reverse every closed door to open heaven in the name of Jesus.

52. Marine curse against my life backfire in the name of Jesus.

53. Serpentine curse against my life, backfire in the name of Jesus.

54. I recover hundred fold what I lost through curse in the dream

55. I shall make it and rise and shine in the name of Jesus.

56. I shall not waste away, but fulfil my destiny on earth in the name of Jesus.

57. My glory shall not go down the grave but explode in the name of Jesus.

58. Let evil thought of the enemy against me melt away in the name of Jesus.

59. Anointing to live holy, flow upon me in the name of Jesus.

60. Any area of my life cursed not to excel, I command you to move forward by fire in the name of Jesus.

61. Even in the face of adversity no strand of my hair shall lost in the name of Jesus.
62. What I gather to promote my life shall not scatter by curse in the dream in the name of Jesus.
63. Anointing of God, deliver me from evil pronouncement
64. I shall not be defeated; my enemy shall fail in the name of Jesus.
65. O Lord, empower me to live righteous life in the name of Jesus.
66. O Lord, let your eye guide me from evil
67. Every foundational curse, break in the name of Jesus.
68. O God arise, let my tears expire in the name of Jesus.
69. I immunize myself with heavenly garment against curse of darkness
70. My head shall not reject blessing in the name of Jesus.
71. Doors of opportunities open to my life in the name of Jesus.
72. I enter and occupy place of peace in the name of Jesus.
73. O Lord, I thank you for cancelling curse of the enemy upon my life.

CHAPTER 9

IF YOU RECEIVE STRANGE KNOCK ON THE HEAD IN THE DREAM

It is a witchcraft manipulation and agenda of darkness for a strange hand to give you Satanic hard knock on the head in the dream. Such knock is loaded with evil mission. The earlier it is addressed, the better.

A knock on the head signifies attack on your destiny. It foretells arrow of insanity, arrow of confusion, power of waste on the loose, disappointment and failure in the offing. It portends arrow of sudden death, instability and inability to fulfil a dream. It is a serious matter and wickedness that open gateway to poverty and agony. Before you know it, victims may have a field day with spirit of poverty.

The intention of every strange power to knock you on the head in the dream is to rubbish your talent. He knows, when your talent is attacked you won't make a head way, but languish in the hands of slave master.

A knock on the head in the dream is therefore what you should not expect to happen. Many have been oppressed this way, many have been under serious groan, while many dwell in the valley.

It is time to cry to God for deliverance, protection and release from evil powers that oppress souls in the dream.

THE WAY OUT

1. Belief in the existence of dream. It is what you belief in, you will trust and be serious about.
2. You need to go for deliverance in this type of situation. Look for a living church that belief in deliverance and does it.
3. Live a life devoid of sin. Conquer sin by revolting against bad habit.
4. Pray to God for a loaded wisdom from the heavenly to boost your thinking faculty.
5. Speak life to every dead organ in your body.
6. It is good you go for counsel in a living church versed in the Word and dreams
7. Command powers behind your predicament to paralyze and die
8. Prophesy good things upon your head
9. Pray that owner of evil load should carry his load

10. Pray that evil hands stretched against you should wither and paralyze

11. Don't be demoralized, awake your inner mind, define your ambition and invest in your growth to attain it; after all, the laws of equity says, "What you sow is what you reap"

12. Pray for divine intervention

13. Use blood of Jesus to cleanse and purify every pollution and evil deposit in your life

14. Be a fearless prayer warrior. Pray all the time, address your situation one by one.

15. Read the Word. If you read your Bible and do what it tells you, Satan will not have field day in your life

16. Read good Christian books, deliverance books, fire prayer books and dream books that will elevate you.

BIBLICAL GUIDELINE

1. Bible Reading: Genesis 3

2. Bible Reference: Judges 5:26

> *"She put her hand to the nail, and her right hand to the workmen's hammer; and with the hammer she smote Sisera, she smote off his head, when she had pierced and stricken through his temple".*

3. Positive Confession: Psalm 27:6

    "And now shall mine head be lifted up above mine enemies round about me: therefore, will I offer in his tabernacle sacrifices of joy; I will sing, yea, I will sing praises unto the LORD".

4. Champion prayer: My head be lifted up above my enemies in the name of Jesus. Amen.

5. Fasting: 6am – 6pm

6. Time for prayer: 12pm – 3am

7. Duration for prayer: 14 days fasting and prayer.

PRAYER POINTS

1. Lord Jesus, preserve me from the fear of the enemy in the name of Jesus.

2. Lord Jesus, protect me from the attack of the enemy in the name of Jesus.

3. O Lord, lift my head above my enemy in the name of Jesus.

4. O Lord, let evil plantation of the enemy upon my head wither to the root in the name of Jesus.

5. O Lord, let the plot of the wicked upon my life scatter, in the name of Jesus.

6. O Lord, let the wicked be consumed by the destruction he plan for me

7. O Lord, let help flow from your sanctuary upon my life, in the name of Jesus.

8. Empower me Lord to subdue enemies of my soul in the name of Jesus.

9. O Lord, anoint my head with oil of breakthrough in the name of Jesus.

10. O Lord, forgive me every sin that will not make my prayer answered in the name of Jesus.

11. Lord Jesus, lead me in your righteousness.

12. O Lord, let my head become danger zone and a "no go area" to my enemy

13. Lord Jesus, reverse Satanic knock on the head that leads to insanity

14. Lord Jesus, reverse Satanic knock on the head that lead to blindness in the name of Jesus.

15. Lord Jesus, reverse satanic knock on the head that leads to sickness in the name of Jesus.

16. Lord Jesus, reverse every dark knock on the head assign to cause failure in my life

17. Owner of evil load, carry your load in the name of Jesus.

18. Every dark cloud around my life, clear away in the name of Jesus.

19. Angel of God cast out my enemies and drag them on the floor, in the name of Jesus.

20. Every plan of the enemy militating against my success, scatter in the name of Jesus.

21. Every attack on my destiny, scatter in the name of Jesus.

22. Every agenda of darkness to scatter my destiny, die in the name of Jesus.

23. Witchcraft manipulation against my destiny, scatter in the name of Jesus.

24. Every evil mission to sink my life; scatter in the name of Jesus.

25. Every arrow of insanity fired into my life; backfire in the name of Jesus.

26. Every arrow of poverty fired into my life; backfire in the name of Jesus.

27. Every arrow of backwardness fired into my life; backfire in the name of Jesus.

28. Every arrow of sickness, fired into my life, backfire in the name of Jesus.

29. Every arrow of confusion fired into my life; backfire in the name of Jesus.

30. Every arrow of failure fired into my life; backfire in the name of Jesus.

31. Every arrow of untimely death fired into my life; backfire in the name of Jesus.

32. Every power assign to rubbish my talent, die in the name of Jesus.

33. Pack of sin in my hands, I throw you away, catch fire and roast to ashes

34. Bad habit that draws Satan to my life, die in the name of Jesus.

35. Anti-miracle spirit in my life, die in the name of Jesus.

36. Wasters assign against my life, die in the name of Jesus.

37. Worldliness in my life, die in the name of Jesus.

38. Every power behind my problem, die in the name of Jesus.

39. I soak my head with blood of Jesus against evil attack

40. Enemies that vow I will lick dust, shall replace me and lick dust, in the name of Jesus.

41. Enemies that surround me about scatter in the name of Jesus.

42. Let the hands of the wicked stretched against me wither in the name of Jesus.

43. Let the head of the dragon that rise against me break, in the name of Jesus.

44. Let my hands be at war against every attack against me in my dream in the name of Jesus.

45. Let the boast of Goliath against me become empty in the name of Jesus.

46. Let the desire of the enemy upon my life, fail woefully in the name of Jesus.

47. Let my enemy go into dead sleep and wake no more in the name of Jesus.

48. Let the habitation of my enemy be desolate in the name of Jesus.

49. Let horrible tempest be the portion of my enemy in the name of Jesus.

50. Let the vigour of enemy against me be deflated, in the name of Jesus.

51. Every embargo upon my head, scatter in the name of Jesus.

52. Lord Jesus, let my life overflow with joy in your name

53. Lord Jesus, let my life overflow with breakthrough in your name

54. Lord Jesus, let my head become power house for breakthrough, in the name of Jesus.

55. I recover every gift I lost as a result of Satanic knock on my head in the name of Jesus.

56. I shall not languish in the hand of slave master in the name of Jesus.

57. I move from state of poverty and want to wealth and glory in the name of Jesus.

58. I shall not swim in murky water of confusion in the name of Jesus.

59. I reverse impossibility in my life to possibility, in the name of Jesus.

60. I reverse every insufficiency in my undertaking to sufficiency in the name of Jesus.

61. Working wonders of God, locate me by fire in the name of Jesus.

62. O Lord, broaden my thinking in the name of Jesus.

63. When trouble besiege me, it shall scatter in the name of Jesus.

64. When trials come my way, they shall fail in the name of Jesus.

65. As East is far from West, so shall problem will be far from me in the name of Jesus.

66. As North is far from South, so shall problem will be far from me in the name of Jesus.

67. Fountain of joy, spring up in my life in the name of Jesus.

68. O Lord, let your favour and mercy be upon me till eternity in the name of Jesus.

69. At last, I laugh my enemies to scorn, thank you Jesus.

CHAPTER 10

IF YOU SEE YOUR CORPSE OR OBITUARY IN THE DREAM

To dream you are dead in the dream foretells tragedy and untimely death in the offing. Anyone fired arrow of death must wake up and pray against it, cancel it and reverse it. Powers behind it must be given serious counter attack.

A dream like this is awful and fearful. It depresses and weakens the soul. The mere fact that you dream this may cause heart attack. No one hears or knows the day of his death and be happy. It is always a day of sorrow. To see your corpse or obituary in the dream foretells disaster in the offing.

The fact is, death is strong. It is the king of terrors and the terror of Kings. Death is a mighty leveller. We are all equal in the presence of death. Death breaks heart, inflict wounds and leave behind trade mark of sorrow and regret. Being ignorant of bad dreams amount to sleep suicide.

People that dream this type of dream may go to bed hale and hearty but never wake the following morning. This is the reason; you must not treat a dream like this with kid gloves. It is a serious matter that must be addressed with all seriousness.

THE WAY OUT

1. When you dream like this, don't treat it with kid's glove. Rise up and cancel it. Belief that dream is real, be serious about it.

2. You must not only cancel such dream but reject it out rightly.

3. Be a born again Christian and invite Jesus into your life. With Jesus on your side untimely death shall be far from you

4. Live a sinless life. This may be difficult to achieve but live a life close to it. Sin invites trouble, it destroys life

5. Always cover yourself with blood of Jesus when you pray before going to bed, and when you pray in the morning after sleep. This shall ward off activities of power of darkness against your life.

6. Read the word and prophesy life, unto your life

7. Be a prayer warrior, all the time. If you pray without ceasing, you will harvest joy and long life.

8. Ask for divine favour, mercy and grace of God to flow you in life. Favour of God shall make you be at the right place, at the right time.

9. Read Christian living books. My book Prayer against Untimely Death shall be of immense help at this material time. Pray the prayers and see what the Lord shall do.

Also, buy my book titled Dictionary of Dreams to give you insight into dreams and interpretations. The book has about ten thousand dreams and interpretations. It is simple to digest and good for home use.

BIBLICAL GUIDELINE

1. Bible Reading: Psalm 18
2. Bible Reference: Psalm 89:48

   "What man is he that liveth, and shall not see death? Shall he deliver his soul from the hand of the grave? Selah".

3. Positive Confession: John 11:43-44

   43. *"And when he thus had spoken, he cried with a loud voice, Lazarus, come forth.*

   44. *And he that was dead come forth, bound hand and foot with grave clothes, and his face was bound about with a napkin. Jesus*

> *saith unto them, "Loose him, and let him go"*

4. Champion prayer: I am loosed from the grip of death in the name of Jesus.

5. Fasting: 6am – 6pm

6. Time for prayer: 12pm – 3am

7. Duration for prayer: 14days fasting and prayer.

PRAYER POINTS

1. O Lord, be my rock and my fortress till eternity in the name of Jesus.

2. O Lord, don't abandon me to the grave in the name of Jesus.

3. O God arise, save me from my enemies in the name of Jesus.

4. O Lord, hear me as I call you in time of distress in the name of Jesus.

5. O Lord, shake and destroy foundations of mountains that rise against me in the name of Jesus.

6. O Lord, save me from powers that threaten me with death

7. O Lord, make my adversaries bow at my feet in the name of Jesus.

8. O Lord, deliver me from the attacks of the enemy, in the name of Jesus.

9. O Lord, save me from violent men, ready to consume me in the name of Jesus.

10. Storm of destruction appear in the camp of the enemy in the name of Jesus.

11. Every gathering against my destiny, scatter in the name of Jesus.

12. Every demonic information used to destroy me, scatter in the name of Jesus.

13. Evil anointing upon my life, dry up in the name of Jesus.

14. Every torrent of destruction against me, scatter in the name of Jesus.

15. Every cord of death that entangle me, break in the name of Jesus.

16. Every cord of the grave that coil around me, break in the name of Jesus.

17. Snores of death that confront me in the dream, die in the name of Jesus.

18. Every arrow of untimely death fired against me, backfire in the name of Jesus.

19. Every arrow of fear fired against me in the dream, backfire in the name of Jesus.

20. Every arrow of sickness fired against me in the dream, backfire in the name of Jesus.

21. Every arrow of poverty fired against me in the dream, backfire in the name of Jesus.

22. Every arrow of disaster fired against me in the dream, backfire in the name of Jesus.

23. Every arrow of sorrow fired against me in the dream, backfire in the name of Jesus.

24. Wounds I sustain as a result of evil arrow in the dream, be healed in the name of Jesus.

25. Every herbal power fashioned against my life, die in the name of Jesus.

26. Grave diggers assign for my sake in the spirit, die in the name of Jesus.

27. Grave diggers enter the grave you dig and be consumed by it, in the name of Jesus.

28. Grave diggers assign for my sake, fight yourselves with the instruments in your hands and die.

29. Every poster of my obituary in the dream, I tear to piece in the name of Jesus.

30. Every poster of my obituary in the dream, catch fire and roast to ashes in the name of Jesus.

31. Thou spirit of death, you shall not level me in the grave in the name of Jesus.

32. Television of darkness assign to announce my obituary, break in the name of Jesus.

33. Television of darkness assign to show my corpse in the dream, break to pieces

34. Thou dark television caster, die in the name of Jesus.

35. I reject bad dream that torment my soul in the name of Jesus.

36. Grave garment assign for me in the dream, catch fire and roast to ashes in the name of Jesus.

37. Oppressors of the dark, die in the name of Jesus.

38. Every affliction assign against me, die in the name of Jesus.

39. Power of death upon my life, die in the name of Jesus.

40. Witchcraft power assign to feed me to death, die in the name of Jesus.

41. O Lord, empower me to live with clean hands, in the name of Jesus.

42. O Lord, empower me to keep away from sin in the name of Jesus.

43. Blood of Jesus, cleanse every mark of untimely death in my body in the name of Jesus.

44. Lord Jesus, forgive me of sins that attach death to my life in the name of Jesus.

45. Power of the dog assign to consume me, die in the name of Jesus.

46. Altar of darkness, where my name is mention for evil, catch fire and roast to ashes in the name of Jesus.

47. O Lord, pull me out of hidden grave in the name of Jesus.

48. Let my persecutors be persecuted, in the name of Jesus.

49. O Lord, I cry unto you for help, help me by fire in the name of Jesus.

50. O Lord, keep my lamp burning and let my soul be far from the grave

51. O Lord, turn darkness in my life to light in the name of Jesus.

52. O Lord, let the camp of the enemy scatter in the name of Jesus.

53. I silence initiators of evil propaganda in the name of Jesus.

54. I pursue, overtake and destroy enemy of my soul in the name of Jesus.

55. I possess heavenly sword and cut enemies of my soul to pieces in the name of Jesus.

56. I possess heavenly arrow and subdue my enemy in the name of Jesus.

57. I bury every failure assign to empty me in the name of Jesus.

58. I bury frustration assign to hasten me to the grave in the name of Jesus.

59. I bury backwardness assign to halt my life, in the name of Jesus.

60. I bury sickness assign to swallow my health in the name of Jesus.

61. Let earth tremble and quake for my sake in the name of Jesus.

62. Let my enemy tremble before me in the name of Jesus.

63. Let me pursue my enemies, overtake and destroy them in the name of Jesus.

64. Let my enemy fall before my feet in the name of Jesus

65. Let me beat my enemies as fine as dust borne in the wind in the name of Jesus.

66. Let great victory be my portion in the name of Jesus.

67. Let the violence of the enemy be shattered in the name of Jesus.

68. The hand of the wicked shall not prosper in my life in the name of Jesus.

69. Let the teeth of evil lion assign to devour me break in the name of Jesus.

CHAPTER 11

IF YOU ARE FIRED ARROW OR BULLET IN THE DREAM

Brethren, you are welcome to this topic that affects life on a daily basis. This topic is an eye opener to bad dreams that kill destiny. It is a dream that affect the foundation of life. You hardly see bad dream that comes into manifestation without an arrow being fired.

Witchcraft powers belief they have license to kill and destroy, and that the best way to do this, is to fire the victims with arrow or bullet in the dream. It is therefore, a disaster to be fired arrow in the dream. They target people with good star in the family or the bread winner, causing fatal injury in the major artery of family biological system.

Evil arrow is deadly, it scatters and bury good destiny. It destroys good things of life, with resultant effect of obstacle, stagnancy, untimely death, career failure, prayerlessness etc. in a life. Evil arrows come in different forms, shapes and names. They include among others, arrow of stagnancy, arrow of failure, arrow of bareness, arrow of sickness and disease, arrow of insanity and arrow of paralysis. Dark arrow in the dream must be addressed fast, so that you are not caught hands down.

THE WAY OUT

We shall enumerate a number of what to do, to silence wicked activity of evil arrow, and what to do, to return evil arrow back to sender. The ways out are many, but we shall discuss salient points below.

1. Give your life to Christ. You hardly excel as a Christian without Jesus. He is the pillar you can rest upon and be sure of safety

2. The basic way out is that you must believe that dream is important in your life. Those who don't dream, or dream and forget their dreams live in the cloud. They are denied things of the spirit in the sleep. This is dangerous. If you fall into this category I implore you to buy my book titled "Prayer to Remember Dreams

3. Be prayerful and be prayer conscious. Pray right prayer against bad dreams. If you suspect it is evil arrow, return the arrow back to sender

4. Pray for grace and mercy of God to be upon you. With mercy of God you shall excel in your undertaking

5. Pray that arrow of God should scatter wicked gathering assign to fire you evil arrow against you

6. Read the word and marry yourself to it. Let the Holy Bible be your spiritual partner. It is the royal Christ in which Jesus ride

7. Confess your sin and quit it. Sin forms wall between you and God and without the presence of God in your life, Satan will have a field day

8. Always cover yourself with pool blood of Jesus, before you go to bed and after you wake from sleep

9. In prayer, pull out every evil arrow in your body

10. Command every dark power behind your predicament to paralyze, ineffective and useless

11. Tell God to empower you in your sleep against powers of darkness

12. Pray together as a family with your spouse and children

PRAYER POINTS

1. O God arise, equip me with arrow proof garment, in the name of Jesus

2. O Lord, paralyze and destroy powers assign to fire evil arrow against me, in the name of Jesus

3. O Lord, let powers that gather against me scatter in the name of Jesus

4. O Lord, let every arrow fired against me go back to sender and consume the sender, in the name of Jesus

5. O Lord, let every hand raised against me wither, in the name of Jesus

6. O Lord, let every power behind my problem paralyze, in the name of Jesus

7. O Lord, let evil agenda of the enemy against me scatter in the name of Jesus

8. O Lord, let evil kingdom that rise against me scatter in the name of Jesus

9. O Lord, let your grace and favour be upon me, in the name of Jesus

10. O Lord, let me be a conqueror in my sleep, in the name of Jesus

11. Every arrow of failure fired against me, backfire in the name of Jesus

12. Every arrow of bareness fired against me, backfire in the name of Jesus

13. Every arrow of fear fired against me, back fire in the name of Jesus

14. Every arrow of ill-luck fired against me, back fire in the name of Jesus

15. Every arrow of untimely death fired against me, backfire in the name of Jesus

16. Every arrow of sickness and disease fired against me, back fire in the name of Jesus
17. Every arrow of rise and fall fired against me back fire in the name of Jesus
18. Every arrow of stagnancy fired against me back fire in the name of Jesus
19. Every arrow of disaster fired against me back fire in the name of Jesus
20. Every arrow of closed door fired against me backfire in the name of Jesus
21. Every arrow of paralysis fired against me back fire in the name of Jesus
22. Every arrow of setback fired against me back fire in the name of Jesus
23. Every arrow of prayerlessness fired against me backfire in the name of Jesus
24. Every arrow of backwardness fired against me back fire in the name of Jesus
25. Every arrow of agony fired against me back fire in the name of Jesus
26. Every arrow of sorrow fired against me back fire in the name of Jesus
27. Every arrow of famine fired against me back fire in the name of Jesus
28. Every arrow of insanity fired against me back fire in the name of Jesus

29. Every arrow of shame and disgrace fired against me back fire in the name of Jesus

30. Every arrow of blindness fired against me, back fire in the name of Jesus

31. Every arrow of nakedness fired against me, back fire in the name of Jesus

32. Every arrow of poverty fired against me, back fire in the name of Jesus

33. Every evil arrow fired from occult kingdom, back fire in the name of Jesus

34. Every evil arrow fired from the pit of hell, backfire in the name of Jesus

35. Every arrow fired from unfriendly friend's back fire in the name of Jesus

36. Every arrow fired from my father's house against my destiny back fire in the name of Jesus

37. Every arrow fired from my mother's house against my destiny back fire in the name of Jesus

38. Every arrow fired from my in-laws' house against my household, back fire in the name of Jesus

39. Every evil arrow fired from other religion against my destiny, back fire in the name of Jesus

40. Every evil arrow fired from evil prophets and fake men of God, backfire in the name of Jesus
41. Every arrow fired from evil wind against my destiny back fire in the name of Jesus
42. Every arrow fired from the grave in order to kill me, backfire in the name of Jesus
43. Every arrow fired to amputate me, backfire in the name of Jesus
44. Every arrow fired to seal heaven against me backfire in the name of Jesus
45. Every arrow fired to destroy my academic progress, my life is not your candidate, back fire in the name of Jesus
46. Every arrow that causes accident fired against me, backfire in the name of Jesus
47. Every arrow fired to make me deaf and dumb, backfire in the name of Jesus
48. Every arrow fired against me, to make me labour without harvest, backfire in the name of Jesus
49. Every arrow that emanates from my foundation, your time is up, die in the name of Jesus
50. Every serpentine arrow fired against me, back fire in the name of Jesus
51. Ever arrow that emanates from masquerade spirit fired against me, back fire in the name of Jesus

52. Every marine spirit arrow fired against me, back fire in the name of Jesus

53. Every arrow fired to cause me to sin backfire in the name of Jesus

54. Every arrow of pollution fired to pollute my destiny backfire in the name of Jesus

55. Every arrow fired to cause me and my family to cry, backfire in the name of Jesus

56. Every arrow of rejection fired against me backfire, in the name of Jesus

57. Every arrow fired to cause barrier between me and my breakthrough backfire in the name of Jesus

58. Every evil arrow lodged in my body come out and die in the name of Jesus

59. Lord Jesus, incubate me with your blood against evil arrow in the name of Jesus

60. Every evil arrow lodged in my body come out and die in the name of Jesus

61. Lord Jesus, empower me to quit sin, I cannot do it alone, help me

62. Lord Jesus, empower me to quit idolatry, I cannot do it alone, help me

63. O Lord, let good news and breakthrough swallow my problem in the name of Jesus

64. O Lord, let me swim in your mercy, favour and grace

65. Wound of evil arrow in my body be healed by the power in the blood of Jesus

66. Season of unlimited joy you are welcome to my house, I say, "Welcome and reside" in the name of Jesus

67. Kingdom of darkness shall not rule over me again in the name of Jesus

68. Henceforth, I shall sing to the Lord songs of joy and victory in the name of Jesus

69. As from now on, all generations shall call me blessed, in the name of Jesus

70. As the mountains surround Jerusalem, so shall the Lord surround me with his angels, in the name of Jesus.

CHAPTER 12

IF YOU ARE PULLED DOWN FROM GREAT HEIGHT IN THE DREAM

There are unseen hands and powers that do evil in the spirit. When enemies try all means to destroy a man and fail, they will allow their target climb to a great height and eventually pull him down. They find it easy to accomplish because their victim felt he is secure and eventually relax. At this point, he may have relaxed in prayer, relax to attend church service or swim in sin. A crack in the wall allows lizard entrance. Hence, an opportunity to strike is open, and thus, Satan strikes. Before you know it, a man previously in high position falls to the bottom of ladder of life.

Anyone so pulled down this way feels disgraced and unfulfilled. He is gripped with fear and agony. He will eventually lose power of command he enjoyed in the past, at home and in office. They suddenly become subject of ridicule among friends and neighbours. How will it be for a vice chancellor of a university to be a gate keeper in same college, or a Managing Director of a company downgraded to be a security officer, managing entrance gate of the same company?

Such situation can best be described as sad and horrible.

In the spirit, to be pulled down from a great height or from exalted position suggest, demotion, stagnation, backwardness, anti-breakthrough forces at work, arrow of failure in the offing, disgrace and anger. Hence, you must find a way out, if you have this type of dream.

THE WAY OUT

1. To behave as if there is no bad dream to contend with is like living in fool's paradise. You must belief in dream and handle it wisely.
2. Make sacrifice and follow it up. Your sacrifice must be total. The position you see yourself in the dream is bad. Sacrifice is not a honey moon. Those who desire honey must be ready to boldly travel down Sacrifice Boulevard!
3. Pull down and scatter every witchcraft embargo placed upon your life so that your heaven may open
4. Accelerate your prayer life, graduate from being a prayer warrior to a prayer warlord to surmount powers of darkness. Pray until the storm is over

5. Break every curse troubling your soul, go for deliverance in a fire prayer church that believe in it

6. Go for counsel in a living church, not one that will tell you to bring cork, sheep, or goat for sacrifice, or bath in the river side

7. Go out with people or friends loaded with wisdom

8. Pursue what is nutritious to your future. Plan for your future and invest in your growth. If you want to get more out of life, you must be prepare to vote more to life

9. Command spirit of poverty in your life to die

10. Pray for divine intervention. Take your case to the court of God and employ Jesus as your Advocate

11. Cover yourself and your property with pool blood of Jesus

12. Avoid sin and quit it. The righteous are protected by God

13. Break every yoke that may settle you at the bottom of the ladder of life

14. Read the Word, your Holy Bible. Always make reference to it and know verses that relate to your needs by heart

15. Read good Christian books that will elevate you spiritually. For details of dream interpretation

buy my book titled "Dictionary of dreams. Also buy, Fire for Fire prayer book to tackle situation like this. For breakthrough prayers buy Discover gold and build wealth.

BIBLICAL GUIDELINE

1. Bible Reading: Deuteronomy 32
2. Bible Reference: Esther 6:12-13

   12.*"And Mordecai came again to the King's gate. But Haman hasted to his house mourning and having his head covered.*

   13.*And Haman told Zeresh his wife and all his friends everything that had befallen him. Then said his wise men and Zeresh is wife unto him, if Mordecai be of the seed of the Jews, before whom thou hast begun to fall, thou salt not prevail against him, but shalt surely fall before him"*

3. Positive confession: Isaiah 40:31

   "But they that wait upon the LORD shall renew their strength; they shall mount up with wings as eagles, they shall run, and not be weary, and they shall walk, and not faint"

4. Champion prayer: By the power of the Living God I shall not be pulled down in the name of Jesus.
5. Fasting: 6am – 6pm
6. Time of prayer: 12pm – 3am
7. Duration of Prayer: 14 days fasting and prayer

PRAYER POINTS

1. O Lord, fight my battle to the end in the name of Jesus
2. O Lord, forgive me of sins that will allow enemy to pull me down in the name of Jesus.
3. Blood of Jesus, cleanse me of filth in my soul and body in the name of Jesus
4. God of Elijah, cut to pieces evil hands assign to pull me down in the name of Jesus
5. Evil hand stretched to pull me down wither in the name of Jesus
6. Witchcraft embargo placed upon my life scatter in the name of Jesus
7. Yoke of darkness upon my life break in the name of Jesus
8. Yoke of stagnancy upon my life, break, in the name of Jesus
9. Yoke of failure in my life, break, in the name of Jesus

10. Every curse pronounced against my life break and back fire in the name of Jesus

11. Every cloud that gather against my future, scatter in the name of Jesus

12. Foolish ideas in me die, in the name of Jesus

13. O Lord, contend with those who contend with my glory in the name of Jesus

14. Let those who seek my life be put to shame in the name of Jesus

15. Every crack in the wall of my life I mend you with blood of Jesus

16. Arrow of disgrace fired against me in order to pull me down, back fire in the name of Jesus

17. Arrow of failure fired against me in order to pull me down, backfire in the name of Jesus

18. Arrow of backwardness fired against me in order to pull me down back fire in the name of Jesus

19. Arrow of sickness fired against me in order to pull me down backfire in the name of Jesus

20. Arrow of untimely death fired against me in order to pull me down backfire in the name of Jesus

21. Arrow of insanity fired against me in order to pull me down backfire in the name of Jesus

22. Arrow of sorrow fired against me in order to pull me down backfire in the name of Jesus

23. Arrow of fear fired against me in order to pull me down, backfire in the name of Jesus

24. Arrow of demotion fired against me in order to pull me down, back fire in the name of Jesus

25. Arrow of stagnation, fired against me in order to pull me down, back fire in the name of Jesus

26. Those that scale the wall in order to pull me down, fall down and die in the name of Jesus

27. Those on chariots in order to pull me down, scatter in your chariot in the name of Jesus

28. Those that sit in high place to pull me down, scatter in the name of Jesus

29. Those who are my peers and are bent in pulling me down meet double failure in the name of Jesus

30. Those that conspire together in order to pull me down, receive judgment of God

31. Those that make spell to pull me down become deaf and dumb in the name of Jesus

32. Those that mock me in order to pull me down, be disgraced in the name of Jesus

33. Those that visit herbalists in order to pull me down, die on your way in the name of Jesus

34. Those that visit fake pastors and alfas in order to pull me down, meet double failure by fire

35. O Lord, heap calamities upon my enemies in the name of Jesus

36. O Lord, take vengeance on my enemy in the name of Jesus
37. O Lord, strike my foes until they rise no more, in the name of Jesus
38. Those who seek my downfall shall fall down flat and be disgraced in the name of Jesus
39. The net enemy prepare for me shall catch them in the name of Jesus
40. I shall not bow my head in grief, in the name of Jesus
41. I shall not be mocked in the name of Jesus
42. The wicked who plot against me shall meet double failure, in the name of Jesus
43. Every disaster fashion against me shall scatter in the name of Jesus
44. O Lord, drive out my enemy before me, in the name of Jesus
45. O Lord, let my strength equal my days, in the name of Jesus
46. Lord Jesus, load me with wisdom in the name of Jesus
47. Listen O heavens, let my enemy be disgraced in the name of Jesus
48. Listen O heavens, send my enemy on journey of no return, in the name of Jesus
49. Listen O heavens, let me be above and not below, in the name of Jesus

50. Listen O heavens, make me the head and not below, in the name of Jesus

51. Listen O heavens, let my attackers, fail woefully, in the name of Jesus

52. Listen O Heavens, let my breakthrough fall like rain, in the name of Jesus

53. Unwise people shall not surround me in the name of Jesus

54. Elders with wisdom locate me for good in the name of Jesus

55. I shall not relax for enemy to pull me down in the name of Jesus

56. O Lord, care for me, in the name of Jesus

57. O Lord, guide me as the apple of your eyes in the name of Jesus

58. O Lord, make me ride on great heights without molestation in the name of Jesus

59. At my feet shall enemies bow, in the name of Jesus

60. I shall not die; neither will my helpers be few in the name of Jesus

61. I will be blessed with the best sun brings forth, in the name of Jesus

62. I will be blessed with the finest moon can yield, in the name of Jesus

63. The sun shall not smite me by day, neither the moon by night, in the name of Jesus

64. To God be the glory, the storm is over in my life in the name of Jesus

65. I am nourished with Lord's honey from the rock, in the name of Jesus

66. I shall not reject the Lord as my saviour, in the name of Jesus

67. My Lord is my shield and helper for ever more. Amen

68. My prayer shall not return to me unanswered, in the name of Jesus

CHAPTER 13

IF YOU EAT FEACES, OR IS POURED ON YOU IN THE DREAM

It is a tragedy if you eat feaces, or is poured on you, in the dream. Feaces stinks and is not meant for consumption. If you feed on it, in the dream, it means there is danger of untimely death, or ill-health and insanity in the offing. Many experience untimely death as a result of this type of attack in the dream. It is a dream that spells negatives in a life. Such person may not live a normal life as his faculty of reasoning is affected from that of a normal being to that of an animal. Poverty takes over such life, as he is reduced to mere chaff in the society.

On the other hand, if feaces is poured on you in the dream, it suggests rejection, pollution, spirit of hatred and poverty. A person so affected may find it difficult to find helpers. He stinks and rejected anywhere he goes. Favour is far from such person. Grace finds no place in him, while mercy never comes his way, he experiences close door wherever he goes as smiles find no place in his face. He looks wretched and pale all the time. Contact with feaces in this way is a tragedy and calamity to existence. May the Lord Almighty bring gap between you and this situation. Amen

THE WAY OUT

1. Don't joke with bad dream, it is real and can come to pass if you treat it with kid's glove
2. Drink blood of Jesus to neutralize and destroy what you consume in the dream
3. Command Holy Ghost power to arrest and kill powers behind your predicament
4. Soak yourself in the pool blood of Jesus, to cleanse you and laminate your body against attacks of darkness
5. Command the hands of power behind your predicament to wither
6. Pray for favour and mercy of God upon you to attract helpers that may have gone elsewhere or refuse to help as a result of attack in your life
7. Tell God to re-build your mind
8. Command closed doors against you to open by fire so that you might possess your possession
9. Be a born again Christian and marry yourself to Christ, he will save you from every predicament
10. Be prayerful, pray all the time and not only when you experience attack in your sleep

11. I advise you go for deliverance in a living church, to right every wrong you went through in the dream

12. Read good Christian books. Apply prayer book like Fire for Fire prayer book in this situation. This book will go a long way to address your situation. Also, buy my book titled Dictionary of dreams so that you might have insight to dreams and interpretations. The book is loaded and has about ten thousand dreams and interpretations.

13. Your Holy bible is a spiritual book that must be your daily food. Read and apply it right.

BIBLICAL GUIDELINE

1. Bible Reading: Psalm 18

2. Bible reference: Psalm 102:9

    "For I have eaten ashes like bread, and mingled my drink with weeping"

3. Positive confession: Psalm 37:10

    "For yet a little while, and the wicked shall not be: yea, thou shall diligently consider his place, and it shall not be"

4. Champion prayer: Dark food assign for me in the spirit, catch fire, and roast to ashes

5. Fasting: 6am – 6pm

6. Time of prayer: 12pm-3am
7. Duration of prayer: 7 days fasting and prayer

PRAYER POINTS

1. Power that want to reduce me to chaff die in the name of Jesus
2. Spirit of insanity assign to attack me die in the name of Jesus
3. Spirit of rejection assign against me die in the name of Jesus
4. Spirit of untimely death, my life is not your candidate therefore die in the name of Jesus
5. Every danger assign for me this year scatter in the name of Jesus
6. Every hand stretched against me wither in the name of Jesus
7. Every garment of rejection in my body, I tear you to pieces and cause you to catch fire in the name of Jesus
8. Occult power assign against my life, die in the name of Jesus
9. Satanic vision for my life, scatter in the name of Jesus
10. Witchcraft power attacking my health die in the name of Jesus

11. Thou wall of sickness that surround me, scatter in the name of Jesus

12. Blood of Jesus, purge me of infirmity in the name of Jesus

13. Blood of Jesus, purge me of affliction in the name of Jesus

14. Blood of Jesus, purge me of evil arrow in the name of Jesus

15. I soak myself in the pool blood of Jesus, to cleanse and destroy filth in my body

16. Bondage of sickness in my life, break in the name of Jesus

17. Every power from the water working against me die in the name of Jesus

18. I dismantle and destroy evil altar built to destroy me in the name of Jesus

19. Sacrifice and rituals assign against me catch fire and roast to ashes in the name of Jesus

20. Messenger of sickness assign to deliver evil message to me die on your way in the name of Jesus

21. Satanic plantation in my life, die to your root in the name of Jesus

22. You legion of sickness and infirmity in my life die in the name of Jesus

23. Battle in my life, scatter in the name of Jesus

24. Arrows of darkness fired against my manifestation backfire in the name of Jesus
25. Every arrow of disgrace fired against me backfire in the name of Jesus
26. Every arrow of poverty fired against me backfire in the name of Jesus
27. Every arrow of stagnancy fired against me backfire in the name of Jesus
28. Every arrow of sorrow fired against me backfire in the name of Jesus
29. O Lord, kill spirit of poverty and lack in my life, in the name of Jesus
30. Every impurity in my body, dry up in the name of Jesus
31. Root of sickness in my blood, wither in the name of Jesus
32. The God who added to the years of Hezekiah shall reverse every negative report about me
33. Powers that stand against my health and wealth die in the name of Jesus
34. Demons behind my problem, your time is up, die in the name of Jesus
35. Environmental pollution in my life, die in the name of Jesus
36. Quencher of greatness in my life die in the name of Jesus

37. Curses on my parents seeking my life, you are a liar, break in the name of Jesus

38. Powers monitoring me for evil die in the name of Jesus

39. Owner of evil load, carry your load in the name of Jesus

40. Powers that determine to put me to shame, you are a liar, die in the name of Jesus

41. Every closed door assign against me open by fire in the name of Jesus

42. Witchcraft bombardment my life is not your candidate, backfire in the name of Jesus

43. Powers that say I will not reach my goal you are not my maker, die in the name of Jesus

44. Strangers in my life, fade away in the name of Jesus

45. Conspiracy against my life scatter in the name of Jesus

46. Every anti-prosperity altar in my father's house, catch fire and roast to ashes in the name of Jesus

47. Every arrow fired into my life as a baby die in the name of Jesus

48. Altar of darkness assign to attack me, catch fire and roast to ashes in the name of Jesus

49. I pull out arrow of the night in my body in the name of Jesus

50. Poison of the enemy in my blood, I flush you out in the name of Jesus

51. Heavenly immunization, cover me against wicked attacks.

52. My soul and body, receive divine healing in the name of Jesus

53. Plans and purpose of God for my life, manifest in the name of Jesus

54. O Lord, pour anointing of favour upon my life in the name of Jesus

55. O Lord, make me candidate of mercy in your kingdom in the name of Jesus

56. Holy Ghost, close gap between me and success in the name of Jesus

57. I laminate and immunize my body with blood of Jesus

58. O Lord, re-shape and re-build me for greatness in the name of Jesus

59. O Lord, let me be a testimony of your work in the name of Jesus

60. I reject vision that says, I will not be delivered in the name of Jesus

61. I proclaim liberty and deliverance over sickness, in the name of Jesus

62. I shall be strong like cedar wood and shall not be shaken in the name of Jesus

63. O Lord, cure me of skin disease enemy ma attack me with, in the name of Jesus

64. I shall not stink before my helpers in the name of Jesus

65. Whatever the situation, I shall rise and shine in the name of Jesus

66. Affliction shall not kill me in the name of Jesus

67. My destiny be healed of spiritual sickness in the name of Jesus

68. Thou storm in my life, be still in the name of Jesus

69. O Lord, clothe me with cloth of grace and strength in the name of Jesus

70. I bind and destroy spirit of hatred from my house in the name of Jesus

71. By your power Lord, favour me when I go out or come in, in the name of Jesus

72. I will not die but live to declare the works of the Lord upon me.

73. O Lord, turn my prayer to testimonies today, in the name of Jesus

CHAPTER 14

IF YOU EAT, SLEEP OR WALK AROUND GRAVE YARD IN THE DREAM

Every dream related to grave yard is dangerous. Grave yard is abode of dead people. Hence, dreams to sleep eat or walk around grave yard foretells arrow of death, and or, spirit of death at rampage. It is synonymous to loss of life or untimely death. Spirits behind such dream is called grave spirit. Such spirit sends people to untimely grave. The same is when you are shown your grave in the dream.

Anything that relates to grave symbolizes destructive agenda in the offing. It foretells mad demons are around to kill and destroy. It is a way of exposing hidden curses about to manifest. Whenever spirit of the grave is on rampage, it is ready to kill, empty purse and cause havoc. I pray that wasters shall not waste your life and property. Amen.

It is high time you speak against spirit that distribute calamity; and reject outright anything that relates to untimely death; as soon as you wake from sleep. Claim your right to live and send evil arrow back to sender. Confront and tell power of the grave that your life is not for sale. Say it loud and clear that grave, and or, grave garment is not your portion. Don't take this dream lightly. Rise up and challenge every spirit that causes untimely death.

THE WAY OUT

1. Belief that dream exposes danger and warning ahead of calamity. Don't joke with your dream. Follow it up.

2. Reject the handwork of spirit of death. Cancel such dream and return evil arrow back to sender

3. Enlist your name in the register of the living in heaven

4. Always cover yourself with blood of Jesus against powers of darkness, whenever they appear to attack, let blood of Jesus appear, to make them flee

5. Call thunder fire of God to consume garment of grave assign for you in the spirit

6. Pray for demarcation and barrier to appear between you and spirit of death

7. Pray violent prayer to cancel such dream. Pray without ceasing and be a prayer warrior

8. Read the Word and apply it to disgrace acts of grave spirit

9. If the dream persists, go for deliverance in a living church
10. Be a born again Christian, and declare yourself child of God that cannot be messed up by dark powers. To be born again, is to be in Christ
11. Read Christian books that will improve your understanding. You can lay hands on my book titled prayer against untimely death. Also, know more of things in the spirit through dreams. Hence, buy my book titled, Dictionary of dreams. This book is an eye opener to dreams and interpretations. It treats over ten thousand dreams and interpretations. Have a copy

BIBLICAL GUIDELINE

1. Bible Reading: Mark 16
2. Bible Reference: Mathew 27:66

   "So they went, and made the sculpture sure, sealing the stone, and setting a watch"

3. Positive Confession: Isaiah 65:20

   "There shall be no more thence an infant of days, nor an old man that hath not filled his days: for the child shall die an hundred years old, but the sinner being an hundred years old shall be accursed"

4. Champion prayer: Grave yard spirit, inviting me to the grave, die in the name of Jesus
5. Fasting: 6am-6pm
6. Time for prayer: 12pm – 3am
7. Duration for prayer: 7days fasting and prayer

PRAYER POINTS

1. O Lord arise, save my soul from power of the grave in the name of Jesus
2. O Lord arise, let grave reject me, in the name of Jesus
3. O Lord arise, let not appetite of the grave enlarge for my sake, in the name of Jesus
4. Lord Jesus, you are Lord over the grave, therefore padlock the mouth of the grave assign to consume me
5. Grave yard, you are the abode of dead people, I am not your candidate, therefore quit my life
6. Thou spirit of death after my life, die in the name of Jesus
8. I receive license to kill, therefore I receive power to kill wicked powers dragging my soul to the grave in the name of Jesus
9. My spirit reverse your step from grave yard, in the name of Jesus

10. Spirit of death in me that makes me walk around grave yard in the spirit, come out of my life and die

11. Powers that invite my spirit to sleep in grave yard, I reject your call, die in the name of Jesus

12. Sleep materials assign for me in grave yard, catch fire and roast to ashes in the name of Jesus

13. Satanic beddings in grave yard assign for me, catch fire and roast to ashes in the name of Jesus

14. Holy Ghost power padlock my mouth from eating food of darkness in the name of Jesus

15. Food of darkness prepared for me in the spirit, catch fire and roast to ashes, in the name of Jesus

16. Dark caterer, assign to prepare food of death for me die in the name of Jesus

17. Dark caterer, carry your evil food, eat it and die in the name of Jesus

18. Evil cutlery assign for me in the spirit, break to pieces in the name of Jesus

19. Dining table of darkness assign for me in the grave yard catch fire and roast to ashes, in the name of Jesus

20. Get together party assign for me in the grave yard, scatter in the name of Jesus

21. Spirit coffin assign for me, catch fire and roast to ashes in the name of Jesus

22. Spirit undertaker assign for my sake, die in the name of Jesus

23. Mourners assign to mourn me, you are not for me, die in the name of Jesus

24. Grave diggers, you are not for me, dig the grave enter, die and be buried in the grave you dig

25. Destiny killers, my life is not for you, die in the name of Jesus

26. Destiny wasters, you shall not waste my life, therefore die in the name of Jesus

27. Ambulance of darkness, assign for me in the spirit, catch fire and roast to ashes in the name of Jesus.

28. O Lord, break the head of the wicked that directs my steps to grave yard

29. Every arrow of death fired against me, backfire in the name of Jesus

30. Every arrow of sorrow fired against me and my household, backfire in the name of Jesus

31. Every arrow of waster fired against me, I fire you back, waste my wasters in the name of Jesus

32. Every arrow of paralysis fired against me backfire, in the name of Jesus

33. Every arrow of sickness fired against me backfire, in the name of Jesus
34. Every arrow of poverty fired against my life, backfire in the name of Jesus
35. Grave spirit, close your mouth by fire, open it no more, in the name of Jesus
36. Satanic gift in my possession catch fire and roast to ashes, in the name of Jesus
37. Every knock of death at my door expire in the name of Jesus
38. Every spirit of death snaring at me, die in the name of Jesus
39. Grave yard spirit, inviting me to the grave die in the name of Jesus
40. Any power that boast I will die before my time, you are not my God, die and replace me in the name of Jesus
41. Every destructive agenda for my sake, scatter in the name of Jesus
42. Every hidden curse against my life, backfire in the name of Jesus
43. Every hidden curse about to manifest, die in the name of Jesus
44. Thou strong man on rampage against my destiny, die in the name of Jesus
45. Wicked power assign to empty my purse, you are a liar, die, in the name of Jesus

46. Garment of grave assign for me catch fire and roast to ashes in the name of Jesus

47. Thou power in custody of grave garment assign for me, die in the name of Jesus

48. Angel of God, seal the grave enemy assign for me in the name of Jesus

49. Embargo of darkness upon my life scatter in the name of Jesus

50. Battles assign to consume me, catch fire and roast to ashes, in the name of Jesus

51. Spirit of vulture against my life die in the name of Jesus

52. Altar of darkness raised against me, catch fire and roast to ashes in the name of Jesus

53. My star, arise and shine, in the name of Jesus

54. Let barrier appear between me and untimely death in the name of Jesus

55. Angel of God, cut the throat of powers assign to kill me, in the name of Jesus

56. I speak failure into the life of powers assign to pull me down in the name of Jesus

57. Enemies shall not run me down, in the name of Jesus

58. I refuse to romance with spirit of death in the name of Jesus

59. I will advance in age to see my great grandchildren in the name of Jesus

60. Calendar of darkness to cut my life short, catch fire and roast to ashes

61. Anointing of old age fall upon me, in the name of Jesus

62. My spirit, reject grave yard spirit, in the name of Jesus

63. My inner man, receive fire, burn to ashes every deposit in my life, in the name of Jesus

64. O Lord, register my name in the book of the living, in the name of Jesus

65. O Lord, cancel my name in the register of the dead, in the name of Jesus

66. Satan, you can't mess me up, therefore quit my life in the name of Jesus

67. My body, it is not time for you to sleep in the grave, therefore receive life by fire

68. I shall fulfill my days on earth in the name of Jesus

69. I shall not die young, in the name of Jesus.

70. I shall live above captivity of darkness in the name of Jesus

CHAPTER 15

IF YOU LOSE YOUR CELL PHONE IN THE DREAM

Cell phone represents your link with God. It is a tragedy if you lose your cell phone in the dream. It is a tragedy in the spirit if you can't link God anymore. It means you are spiritually lonely and powerless before your enemies, as you won't have who to communicate with. This means, you are at the mercy of Satan anytime you lost cell phone in the dream.

In the spirit, telephone represents message from God, counsel, prayer, union, gossip or enemy's voice. If you lose one in the dream, it foretells communication gap with God. Hence, it is a problem if you lose your cell phone in the dream. It calls for prayer and emergency to rescue such situation.

It is in a period like this, dark arrows are fired into a life because you are cut off from God.

If you are right before God and filled with Holy Spirit; you will effectively communicate with God. Your communion with God will be as one talking to a person close by. You contact with God with ease and stress less. But, when you are prayer less and live in sin your voice may not ascend to heaven. It is in such time you may lose your cell phone in the dream.

THE WAY OUT

1. Ensure you count on dreams. Don't treat it with a wave of the hands. Dream is real, and full of communication that must be decoded.
2. You must live a sinless life if you want your voice to be heard in heaven. Our God is holy, and may look elsewhere if you live in sin. Therefore, confess your sins and quit it.
3. Be prayerful. Be a prayer warrior that leaves no stone un-turn in prayer.
4. Always cover yourself and your property with blood of Jesus. By so doing, enemies shall fail to come close to you.
5. If the dream makes you fear, go for deliverance in a living church. Satan fears a prayerful person; he knows he is a loss if you hold on to Christ.
6. Be a born again Christian. Surrender your life to Christ, marry your soul and body to him.
7. Pray and recover your stolen cell phone from powers of darkness holding on to your property.

It is your property, therefore possess your possession.

8. Command every closed door caused as a result of time gap you lost your phone in the spirit, to open by fire.

9. Ask favour of God to flow in your life.

10. Read your Holy Bible for spiritual upliftment and hunger for heaven. When you read and understand the Bible, you shall take the right step in the right direction.

11. Read living Christian books. You can handle every fierce battle with my book titled Fire for Fire, and buy my book titled Dictionary of dreams, so that you might know how to interpret dreams better.

BIBLICAL GUIDELINE

1. Bible Reading: Jeremiah 33.
2. Bible Reference: Psalm 106: 6-7.

> 6. *"We have sinned with our fathers, we have committed iniquity, we have done wickedly.*
>
> 7. *Our fathers understood not thy wonders in Egypt; they remembered not the multitude of thy mercies; but provoked him at the sea, even at the Red Sea".*

3. Positive Confession: Isaiah 1:18.

   "Come now, and let us reason together, saith the LORD: though your sins be as scarlet, they shall be as white as snow; though they be red like crimson, they shall be as wool."

4. Champion Prayer: By his grace, my God has forgiven my sins, and my relationship with him is solid, in the name of Jesus. Amen.

5. Fasting: 6am-6pm.

6. Time of Prayer: 11pm-3am.

7. Duration of Prayer: 9 days fasting and prayer.

PRAYER POINTS

1. Electric current of God, flow in my life, in the name of Jesus.

2. My link with God, open by fire in the name of Jesus.

3. Lord Jesus, this is emergency situation, bail me out in the name of Jesus.

4. Rescue team of heaven, locate me by fire and help me in the name of Jesus.

5. O Lord, turn your ear to me for signs and wonders, in the name of Jesus.

6. Temple of un-holiness in my life be dismantled in the name of Jesus.

7. Mockers of my life, become my servant in the name of Jesus.

8. Marine powers against me, live me alone, in the name of Jesus.

9. Hands that stole my cell phone in the dream wither in the name of Jesus.

10. Every barrier between me and God, break in the name of Jesus.

11. Voice of enemy in my ear, come to end today in the name of Jesus.

12. Anti-Christ powers in my life, be exposed and be disgraced in the name of Jesus.

13. Battle of darkness in my life, scatter in the name of Jesus.

14. Every serpent and scorpion assign to hurt me, you shall fail in your mission in the name of Jesus.

15. God of Elijah, lay your hands of fire upon me, to receive power in the name of Jesus.

16. Wasters of destiny, my life is not your candidate, die in the name of Jesus.

17. Witchcraft unity against me scatter in the name of Jesus.

18. Witchcraft anointing upon my head, dry in the name of Jesus.

19. Witchcraft fire assign to counter fire of God in my life, quench in the name of Jesus.

20. Any power assign to kill my potentials, you are a liar die in the name of Jesus.

21. Any power that boasts, prayer and fasting shall not solve my problem, you are a liar, die in the name of Jesus.

22. Any power, assign to scatter my calling die in the name of Jesus.

23. Every Satanic arrangement to pull me down, scatter in the name of Jesus.

24. Dark arrows fired against my destiny backfire in the name of Jesus.

25. Arrow of prayerlessness fired against me backfire, in the name of Jesus.

26. Every arrow of stagnancy fired against me backfire, in the name of Jesus.

27. Arrow of failure fired into my life, backfire in the name of Jesus.

28. Rituals carried out to harm me, backfire in the name of Jesus.

29. Stubborn pursuer after my life, summersault and die in the name of Jesus.

30. O God arise, arrest my arresters in the name of Jesus.

31. Every power waging war against my peace die, in the name of Jesus.

32. Every agent of darkness, assign to control affairs of my life die in the name of Jesus.

33. Satanic prayer band against my life, scatter in the name of Jesus.
34. Pillar of abomination erected against my destiny, I pull you down in the name of Jesus.
35. Every covenant with failure, break in the name of Jesus.
36. Satanic meeting for my sake, scatter in the name of Jesus.
37. Every closed door against my destiny, open by fire, in the name of Jesus.
38. Powers behind closed door in my life, die in the name of Jesus.
39. Evil harvesters assign to harvest my glory, what do you mean? Die in the name of Jesus.
40. Pillar of darkness around me, I pull you down in the name of Jesus.
41. Pillar of fire, give me divine light and direction in the name of Jesus.
42. Satanic arrangement for my life scatter, in the name of Jesus.
43. Mr. Nobody dwelling in my life die in the name of Jesus.
44. Prayerless spirit in my life, come out and die in the name of Jesus.
45. Dark padlock against my life, break and scatter in the name of Jesus.

46. Powers threatening my foundation, do you know me I am rooted in the rock of ages? Die in the name of Jesus.

47. Drum of war against my destiny, break, catch fire and roast to ashes in the name of Jesus.

48. Blood of Jesus, cover and protect me in the name of Jesus.

49. Sins that will make me lose my connection with God, I do away with you in the name of Jesus.

50. Lord Jesus, build me afresh with power that will cause outbreak of revival in this generation.

51. Spirit to decode dream come upon me in the name of Jesus.

52. Spirit of war, give way to spirit of peace in my life, in the name of Jesus.

53. Satanic petition against me, I tear you to pieces in the name of Jesus.

54. Any power assign to fuel problem in my life die in the name of Jesus.

55. Anointing that will keep me permanently on the top fall upon me in the name of Jesus.

56. Circle of darkness around me clear away in the name of Jesus.

57. Lord Jesus, counsel me on how to excel in life.

58. My ear, be available to message of God, in the name of Jesus.

59. Every attack on message from throne of God, stop by fire, in the name of Jesus.
60. I take my seat from strangers occupying it in the name of Jesus.
61. I cover my spiritual phone with blood of Jesus.
62. Holy Spirit, drag me to mountain top for great testimonies in the name of Jesus.
63. Lord Jesus, fill me with Holy Spirit by fire.
64. O Lord, give me deep hunger for your word in the name of Jesus.
65. No Satanic power shall kill the purpose of God for my life in the name of Jesus.
66. Heavenly transformation, take place in my life, in the name of Jesus.
67. I recover my cell phone by fire in the name of Jesus.
68. My witness to souls shall not be in vain, in the name of Jesus.
69. I will be found in Christ and walk His way, in the name of Jesus.
70. O Lord, I commit all my ways to you, forever more.
71. O Lord, let ministering angels guide me from havoc, in the name of Jesus.
72. Sin shall find no place in my life in the name of Jesus.

73. Praise the Lord; enemy has lost the battle against me in the name of Jesus.

CHAPTER 16

IF YOU SEE YOUR PICTURE IN SEALED BOTTLE IN THE DREAM

Your picture represents you in the spirit. Therefore, if you see your picture in a sealed bottle in the dream foretells you are under captivity. It connotes a life in wilderness, where economy is stagnant, recessed or bad, and or, where infrastructure is fractured.

Don't be surprise, you may end up as a person people come to for assistance, that give in abundance but later find himself finding it difficult to feed but beg before he can feed. Brethren, it may get to a stage where the sick is dying and the dead can't be accorded a befitting burial.

The fact remains, situation may not favour you any longer, as a result of witchcraft bombardments here and there. Money suddenly becomes scarce commodity in your home while heaven closes against you. At this point honey is rear to come by. Enemy's heart is hardened against you. They make future frightful and hopeless in order to establish testament of woe in your life.

I pray, you shall not experience this in the name of Jesus. Amen

THE WAY OUT

1. Pray and command thunder of God to break the evil bottle to pieces so that you may experience deliverance from destiny destroyer.
2. Treat your dream with all seriousness. Believe dream exist and know how to interpret them.
3. Always cover yourself in the pool blood of Jesus before you sleep at night and when you wake in the morning
4. Retrieve your picture in the spirit from evil hands
5. Pray violent prayer to scatter and paralyze evil activities of the enemy
6. Break every embargo placed upon your life in the spirit
7. Live a sinless life and be a born again Christian so that you might not be an easy prey in the hand of Satan
8. Break every covenant your destiny may have been covenanted with in the spirit
9. Read the Word and marry yourself to Holy Bible
10. Go for deliverance in a living church that believes and pray deliverance prayers

11. Read good Christians books. The more you read, better for you. In this situation lay your hands on deliverance prayer book like Fire for Fire, and Dictionary of dream, for better understanding of your dream.

BIBLE GUIDELINE

1. Bible reading: Jeremiah 14
2. Bible Reference: Ephesians 6:11

   "Put on the whole armour of God, that ye may be able to stand against the viles of the devils"

3. Positive Confession: Psalm 18:43

   "Thou hast delivered me from the strivings of the people, and thou hast made me the head of the heathen: a people whom I have not known shall serve me"

4. Champion prayer: Satanic captivity in my life, scatter, in the name of Jesus. Amen
5. Fasting: 6am-6pm
6. Time for Prayer: 12pm – 3am
7. Duration for prayer: 9 days fasting and prayer.

PRAYER POINTS

1. Power of demotion lose your hold upon me in the name of Jesus

2. O God arise, re-package me for wonders in the name of Jesus

3. O God of wonder set me free from captivity of darkness in the name of Jesus

4. Lord Jesus, forgive me, I am sorry for my sins

5. Lord Jesus, nail my sin to the cross and set me free

6. Lord Jesus, pronounce me guiltless before my accuser

7. Lord Jesus, forgive me, I deserve mercy and not sacrifice

8. Powers of darkness that cover my glory die in the name of Jesus

9. Cloud of darkness that cover me clear away in the name of Jesus

10. Wicked works of darkness assign to scatter my destiny expire in the name of Jesus

11. Powers creating diversion in my life, your time is up die in the name of Jesus

12. Powers assign to scatter plans and purpose of God for my life, die in the name of Jesus

13. Every spiritual blindness holding me captive, expire in the name of Jesus

14. Every prison wall that cage me, break in the name of Jesus

15. I throw into dustbin of life, every work of darkness in my hands in the name of Jesus

16. O Lord, deliver me from powers of darkness in the name of Jesus.

17. O Lord, deliver me and my family from the hands of the wicked in the name of Jesus.

18. Evil bottle that cage my glory break in the name of Jesus.

19. Arrow of paralysis fired against me backfire in the name of Jesus.

20. Veil of darkness in my face, I pull you off and cast you to fire of God.

21. Chains of darkness in my hands break in the name of Jesus.

22. Chains of darkness in my legs break in the name of Jesus.

23. Trap of darkness for my life, catch your owner in the name of Jesus

24. Powers of my father's house, I bind you in the name of Jesus.

25. Gate of darkness holding me captive break open in the name of Jesus.

26. Dark cloud causing failure in my life, clear away in the name of Jesus.

27. Evil food I ate in the dream causing failure in my life, die in the name of Jesus.

28. Every dark pronouncement against me backfire in the name of Jesus.

29. Owner of evil load carry your load in the name of Jesus.

30. My eyes see great things of life, turn it to vision and manifestation in the name of Jesus.

31. Every altar of darkness fashion against me catch fire and roast to ashes.

32. Every wicked decision taken against me scatter in the name of Jesus.

33. Every garment of failure in my body, I pull you off in the name of Jesus.

34. Powers dragging me out of house of God be silenced in the name of Jesus.

35. Spiritual burial hanging on my neck die in the name of Jesus.

36. O God arise re-write my history today.

37. Every arrow of darkness fired against me backfire, in the name of Jesus.

38. Arrow of poverty fired against me backfire in the name of Jesus.

39. Arrow of disgrace fired against me backfire in the name of Jesus.

40. Arrow of untimely death fired against me backfire in the name of Jesus.

41. Arrow of stagnancy fired against me backfire in the name of Jesus.

42. Arrow of sickness and diseases fired against me backfire in the name of Jesus.

43. I shall not drink from cup of sorrow in the name of Jesus.

44. I shall not eat from table of sorrow in the name of Jesus.

45. Witchcraft attack against me scatter in the name of Jesus.

46. Blood sucking powers assign to suck my body, my life is not your candidate; die in the name of Jesus.

47. Power of death, my life is not your candidate, reverse your step and die in the name of Jesus

48. Familiar spirit with rod of death to attack me die in the name of Jesus

49. In the journey of life, dark lion shall not devour me in the name of Jesus

50. In the journey of life, death there in shall not kill me, in the name of Jesus

51. In the journey of life, every cage assign for me shall break, catch fire and roast to ashes

52. Every covenant of failure in my life break in the name of Jesus.

53. Doors of breakthrough open in the name of Jesus.

54. Every embargo of darkness holding me captive break; in the name of Jesus.

55. Every embargo of financial loss on my career break, in the name of Jesus.

56. Every embargo of stagnancy placed on me break in the name of Jesus.

57. Every embargo of sickness placed on me break in the name of Jesus.

58. Evil padlock fashion against my finance break in the name of Jesus.

59. Oh heaven open, and favour me in the name of Jesus.

60. The bridge shall not break against helpers of my situation in the name of Jesus

61. Every wound in my heart be healed in the name of Jesus

62. People that look up to me before shall not look down on me in the name of Jesus.

63. Evil record working against me scatter and catch fire in the name of Jesus.

64. I shall overcome errors of the past in the name of Jesus.

65. Those who boast I shall fail shall be the one that will fail in the name of Jesus.

66. Liabilities shall reduce drastically, while my asset shall grow by fire in the name of Jesus.

67. Money shall not be a scarce commodity in my pocket in the name of Jesus.

68. My star, arise and shine in the name of Jesus.

69. The plans and purpose of God for my life shall not be aborted in the name of Jesus

70. The rod and staff of Jesus shall comfort me, I the name of Jesus

71. I thank you, Oh my Lord, I am not on sick bed.

CHAPTER 17

IF YOU LOST KEY IN THE DREAM

This is a terrible dream that must be addressed with urgency. Key in the dream suggest power of authority, instrument that opens closed door, power to march ahead, authority of direction, success at hand. If you hold key in your hand, it means you have authority and power to open closed doors; reverse is the case if you don't hold the right key to a door or gate, or you lost one in the dream.

So, it is dangerous to lose your key in the dream, or if it is stolen or misplaced in the dream. In either case, it boils down to loss of keys in the dream. It is therefore dangerous if your key is lost to thieves or robbers in the dream. Such situation foretells loss of authority over a situation or position, closed door to prosperity, attack that may cause spiritual vacuum in a life, unexpected un-pleasantry in the offing, and or, disappointment ahead.

If you lost key in the dream, barrier and obstacles are created between you and success. Things will naturally go dull, business openings may close, helpers may seize to give helping hands, victim may lose voice of command, yoke may appear or increase in size, spirit of poverty may strike, if you lose your key in the dream.

I pray, you shall find every key of authority and progress, you lost in the dream. Amen

THE WAY OUT

1. To belief in the spirituality of dream is the first step that can make you escape powers inherent in bad dreams. Therefore, belief dream is real and must be rightly interpreted.
2. The first thing is to recover your lost key in the dream, or pray to locate it if you misplaced it in the dream.
3. Always cover yourself and your property with blood of Jesus. If you do, enemy will be powerless over your key, because it would be impossible for enemy to tamper with what blood of Jesus covers.
4. At all times, be a born again Christian. Don't be an 'Epileptic Born Again Christian." Born again today, worldly tomorrow, is not the best. You can't serve mammon and Christ the same time.
5. Pray without ceasing. Be a giant in the spirit against principality and powers. Prayer makes

you a champion powers of darkness cannot contend with, even with your key in the spirit.

6. In order to place permanent end to loss of key in the dream, go for deliverance.

7. Seek counsel from men of God of a living church.

8. Always marry yourself to your Holy Bible, to train you on what to do and step to take through the Holy Spirit.

9. Read Christian based literature that will educate and expose you to things of the spirit. To overcome attack of this nature, use my book titled Fire for Fire prayer book.

Also buy my book Dictionary of dreams, so that you may understand how to interpret dreams accurately.

BIBLICAL GUIDELINE

1. Bible Reading: Isaiah 22.

2. Bible Reference: Romans 13:11-12.

> 11 *"And that, knowing the time, that now it is high time to awake out of sleep: for now is salvation nearer than when we believed.*
>
> 12 *The night is far spent, the day is at hand: let us therefore cast off the works*

of darkness, and let us put on the armour of light."

3. Positive Confession: Isaiah 61:7.

    "For your shame ye shall have double; and for confusion they shall rejoice in their portion: therefore, in their land they shall possess the double: everlasting joy shall be unto them."

4. Champion Prayer: Powers that brings shame to life my life is not your candidate, die, in the name of Jesus.

5. Fasting: 6am-6pm.

6. Time of Prayer: 11pm-2am.

7. Duration of Prayer: 14 days fasting and prayer.

PRAYER POINTS

1. Every danger spot around me clear away in the name of Jesus.

2. Every danger spot before me clear away in the name of Jesus.

3. Every danger spot behind me clear away, in the name of Jesus.

4. Afflictions in my life die, in the name of Jesus.

5. O Lord, blot out the handwriting of the wicked against me in the name of Jesus.

6. Any power assign to tear my garment of authority die in the name of Jesus.

7. Powers assign to cause financial nakedness in my life die in the name of Jesus.

8. Spiritual wilderness in my life, clear away in the name of Jesus.

9. Every trumpet blown against my authority, become soundless, break in the name of Jesus.

10. Drum of war targeted against me, break to pieces in the name of Jesus.

11. Betrayals in the vineyard of my life, be fed with confusion in the name of Jesus.

12. O Lord, give me key of authority to open closed doors against me in the name of Jesus.

13. O Lord, give me power to overcome every disappointment that comes my way in the name of Jesus.

14. Any fake key assign to replace my original key in the dream, catch fire and roast to ashes.

15. Devourers of breakthrough, die in the name of Jesus.

16. Powers that want me to move from hero to zero die, in the name of Jesus.

17. Powers that hunt my parents and are now after me die in the name of Jesus.

18. Spirit of almost there in my body, come out and die in the name of Jesus.

19. Curse of almost there pronounced against me backfire in the name of Jesus.

20. Powers monitoring my breakthrough in the spirit die in the name of Jesus.

21. Powers that determine to destroy me, die in the name of Jesus.

22. Wherever enemies of my progress are, fires of God consume them in the name of Jesus.

23. Every witchcraft decision taken against me in the spirit be nullified in the name of Jesus.

24. Any power, assign to stop my glory from shinning, die in the name of Jesus.

25. Powers that tamper with my destiny die in the name of Jesus.

26. Every closed door to prosperity open by fire in the name of Jesus.

27. Every barrier between me and breakthrough, scatter in the name of Jesus.

28. Every dull situation in my life expire in the name of Jesus.

29. Helpers of my destiny appear and help me by fire in the name of Jesus.

30. My voice of command, roar like thunder in the name of Jesus.

31. Every yoke upon my life, die in the name of Jesus.

32. Spirit of poverty in my life, die in the name of Jesus.
33. I cover my life and property with blood of Jesus.
34. Spirit of epileptic Born Again in my life, die in the name of Jesus.
35. O Lord, deliver my soul from powers of darkness in the name of Jesus.
36. Terrible dreams in my sleep, stop by fire in the name of Jesus.
37. Spiritual battle against my authority scatter in the name of Jesus.
38. Power boasting to turn my life upside down, you are not my maker, die in the name of Jesus.
39. Every mouth reporting me in order to harm me, I tear your mouth to pieces in the name of Jesus.
40. Arrows fired against me at mountain top in order to pull me down, backfire in the name of Jesus.
41. Arrow of prayerlessness fired against me in order to render me useless, backfire in the name of Jesus.
42. Roaring lion against my authority, today is your last day, die in the name of Jesus.
43. Thou foundation of my life, receive deliverance in the name of Jesus.

44. O Lord, deliver me from bondage of sin in the name of Jesus.

45. The sun of my life shall not fade in the name of Jesus.

46. Lord Jesus by your power nail my sin to the cross.

47. My eyes refuse to be darkened by sin.

48. My ears refuse to be darkened by sin.

49. My tongue, refuse to be darken by sin.

50. The door of glory my Father open, enemy shall not close it in the name of Jesus.

51. O Lord, lock every satanic door, enemy open for my sake.

52. My door of favour, open by fire in the name of Jesus.

53. My door of breakthrough, open by fire in the name of Jesus.

54. Every good door I open shall not be taken over by enemy in the name of Jesus.

55. Every feather of my eagle, receive power of excellence in the name of Jesus.

56. The Ark of the Lord shall not depart from my house in the name of Jesus.

57. Anointing of overcomer fall upon me in the name of Jesus.

58. O Lord, pass judgment against my enemy by fire in the name of Jesus.

59. O Lord, give me power to tap from the abundance of your power in the name of Jesus.

60. O Lord, give me divine acceleration to conquer and dominate in the name of Jesus.

61. O Lord, give me grace to be on the top in the name of Jesus.

62. O Lord, give me power and authority to forge ahead in life, in the name of Jesus.

63. My key stolen in the dream, I recover you in the name of Jesus.

64. When sun shines, no one can cover it, therefore no one shall stop me from shining in the name of Jesus.

65. I will rise from minima to maxima level of life in the name of Jesus.

66. I will rise from valley of decay to mountain top of success in the name of Jesus.

67. I will rise from insufficient level to level of abundance in the name of Jesus.

68. I will rise from corridor of power to inner chamber of power God destine for me.

69. Failure, I reject and divorce you in the journey of my life in the name of Jesus.

70. Spiritual nakedness shall not find place in my life in the name of Jesus.

71. Let temple of un-holiness in my life be dismantled in the name of Jesus.

72. No evil harvester shall find place in my life in the name of Jesus.
73. Every Satanic arrangement for my life shall not stand in the name of Jesus.

CHAPTER 18

WHEN PRESSED DOWN IN THE DREAM

To be pressed down in the dream is a witchcraft attack against your destiny. It is one of the ways enemies use to torment and bring agenda of God upon a person to nothing. Their primary aim is to inject delay and impossibility in a life. Such victim will nurse ideas but will never fulfil it. He will struggle on a project but may not see the light of the day. He may nurse ideas but won't do a follow up. Such person jettison plans he so much craved for.

Obstacles and impossibilities appear in the life of such person while catastrophe appears in business, career or calling. Strange things happen that make good things disappear into thin air.

Anyone so affected experience weakness of the body, followed by fear and confusion in the mind. He may not be able to do right thing at the right time, neither will he be focused. To be pressed down in the dream forecasts struggle with no result, as powers that hinder progress are at hand; as a result delay, ill-luck and rejection before helpers become the order of the day.

This is a dream you must handle with all seriousness. It is not an acrobat or picnic exercise. Act now and be delivered of witchcraft attacks.

Witchcraft powers that torment this way, make their victims walk around breakthroughs but never get it. They will see good things ahead but miss it. It is always struggle without achievement.

THE WAY OUT

1. The first way out is to believe that dream is real with meaning.
2. When you have bad dream like this, pray fervently against it. Cancel the dream and return every evil arrow back to sender.
3. Cover yourself with blood of Jesus whenever you go to bed. When Satan sees blood of Jesus in you, he will reverse his step.
4. Drink blood of Jesus to purge you of evil deposit.
5. Recover all you lost as a result of being pressed down in the dream. Anyone pressed down in the dream, lose one or two things in the spirit, as a result of delay, ill-luck and rejection caused by it.

6. Claim your right. Whenever you wake after such experience, claim your right; that God created you to be a leader and not a borrower, the head and not the tail.

7. Read the Word, use the Word, claim the Word as it affects you. The Word shall set you free, if you read and apply it.

8. In your presence before God, confess your sins. Sin allows Satan and his agents to have access to life. Sin is the excuse Satan use to torment us in real life, which starts in the dream.

9. Above all, be a born again Christian. Surrender all to Christ and do his will.

For dream details I recommend my book titled Dictionary of dreams. It is a book each home should have. It has over ten thousand (10,000) dreams and interpretations, with prayer points as well. Go for it.

BIBLICAL GUIDELINE

1. Bible Reading: Psalm 59.
2. Bible Reference: Jeremiah 50:33.

"Thus saith the LORD of hosts, the children of Israel and the children of Judah were oppressed together: and all

that took those captives held them fast; they refused to let them go."

3. Positive Confession: Isaiah 10:1.

    "Woe unto them that decree unrighteous decrees, and that write grievousness which they have prescribed."

4. Champion Prayer: O Lord, break the backbone of those that oppress me in the dream, in the name of Jesus. Amen.

5. Fasting: 6am-6pm.

6. Time of Prayer: 12pm-3am.

7. Duration of Prayer: 7 days fasting and prayer.

PRAYER POINTS

1. O Lord, lift my head above my enemy, in the name of Jesus.

2. Fire of God, surround me every hour of the day, in the name of Jesus.

3. Holy Ghost Power, guide me everywhere I go and in my sleep, in the name of Jesus.

4. I cover myself with blood of Jesus against attack of darkness in the name of Jesus.

5. Every witchcraft attack against my destiny, backfire in the name of Jesus.

6. Powers assign to scatter agenda of God for my life, die in the name of Jesus.

7. Witchcraft power that wants me to live a sorrowful life die, in the name of Jesus.

8. Powers that press me down in the dream, your time is up, die in the name of Jesus.

9. Spirit of procrastination in my life die, in the name of Jesus.

10. Every struggle without achievement in my life, come to an end in the name of Jesus.

11. O Lord, let me live above struggle without result, in the name of Jesus.

12. Powers assign to monitor me into failure, die in the name of Jesus.

13. Every delay and impossibility injected into my life, come out and die in the name of Jesus.

14. Dark powers battling for the control of my life, die in the name of Jesus.

15. Powers that press me down in order to loot me in the dream die, in the name of Jesus.

16. Spirit of delay, assign to destroy my career die in the name of Jesus.

17. Spirit of delay, assign to kill my destiny, die in the name of Jesus.

18. Spirit of delay, assign to cage me in the spirit, die in the name of Jesus.

19. Spirit of delay, assign to pull me down, die in the name of Jesus.

20. Spirit of delay, assign to keep me in the valley of darkness, die in the name of Jesus.
21. Spirit of impossibility boasting I shall not make it in life, die with your boast in the name of Jesus.
22. Every spirit of impossibility that gang up against me, meet double failure in the name of Jesus.
23. Spirit of impossibility in my father's house causing failure in my life, die in the name of Jesus.
24. Good thing that disappear as a result of being pressed down in the dream, appear and locate me in the name of Jesus.
25. Powers that hinder progress in my life die in the name of Jesus.
26. Powers that hinder progress my life is not your candidate die in the name of Jesus.
27. Powers that want me to struggle like an elephant, but eat like ant, you shall fail, die in the name of Jesus.
28. Powers that want me to occupy the tail region of life you are a liar, die in the name of Jesus.
29. Problem developers for my life, die in the name of Jesus.
30. Problem brewers, I paralyze your activity upon my life, in the name of Jesus.

31. Every barrier standing between me and breakthrough scatter, in the name of Jesus.

32. Every strange thing in my life, that make good things fail to happen, die.

33. Every weakness introduced to my body, as a result of being pressed down in the dream die.

34. Fear and confusion in the mind, die in the name of Jesus.

35. Garment of rejection in my life, catch fire and roast to ashes in the name of Jesus.

36. I pull off garment of rejection in my life to acceptance and favour before men and God, in the name of Jesus.

37. I convert rejection in my life to acceptance and favour before men and God, in the name of Jesus.

38. I pull down satanic empire working against my success in the name of Jesus.

39. Every hidden arrow in my body, come out and die in the name of Jesus.

40. Thou instrument of the enemy fashioned against me, be disappointed in the name of Jesus.

41. Those that trouble my Israel shall be troubled, in the name of Jesus.

42. Those that conspire and counsel against me shall fail in the name of Jesus.

43. Opposition against my breakthrough, scatter in the name of Jesus.

44. O Lord, let my heavenly project be fulfilled on earth, in the name of Jesus.

45. I paralyze activities of powers assign to attack me in the dream, in the name of Jesus.

46. Tree of sorrow in my life be uprooted, in the name of Jesus.

47. I bind every spirit of oppression struggling with my destiny, in the name of Jesus.

48. I bind every spirit of heaviness that makes my spirit low, in the name of Jesus.

49. I bind every spirit of slumber that makes sleep without limit, in the name of Jesus.

50. Let owner of evil load carry their load in the name of Jesus.

51. I drink blood of Jesus, to purge and destroy evil deposit in my body in the name of Jesus.

52. I cover myself with blood of Jesus to ward off evil encroachment in my life, in the name of Jesus.

53. Lord Jesus, let your blood flow around me whenever I sleep in the name of Jesus.

54. Lord Jesus, forgive me every sin that allow dark power to oppress me in the name of Jesus.

55. O God arise and fight my battle for me, in the name of Jesus.

56. Every project in my hand, see the light of the day, in the name of Jesus.
57. I shall be the head and not the tail, in the name of Jesus.
58. I shall be lender to nations, and not a borrower in the name of Jesus.
59. I take authority over powers assign to trouble me in the name of Jesus.
60. I unseat evil powers sitting upon my promotion in the name of Jesus.
61. I unseat every dark power sitting upon success in the name of Jesus.
62. I break curses upon my life by the power in the blood of Jesus.
63. I break powers of wasters in my life, in the name of Jesus.
64. I break powers of devourers in my life, in the name of Jesus.
65. O Lord, give me power to do right thing at the right time, in the name of Jesus.
66. Favour of God shall be my portion in the name of Jesus.
67. I shall laugh last over oppressors in my dream in the name of Jesus.
68. My head, refuse bewitchment in the name of Jesus.

CHAPTER 19

IF YOUR CAR BREAK DOWN IN THE DREAM

Automobile makes journey smooth, quick and easy. Motor car in the spirit connotes personality, ministry, business, marital journey etc. Thus, whatever affects your car in the dream may affect you in real life. This is the reason you should not treat dream with kid's glove. It is a serious matter that needs serious attention.

So, if your car breaks down in the dream, it means you must rise to situation fast, as dark powers may constitute nuisance in your business or career. Break down of car in the spirit suggest possible problems like trouble, opposition, delay and hindrance in the offing.

A dream of this nature suggests possible trouble as opposition may arise here and there. Thus, delay and setback is imminent before you can forge ahead. The summary of this is, you need clinical investigative approach in matters you handle at this material time.

Enemies are around to adulterate your honey of life. Therefore, you must sacrifice time and energy to guide your honey in order to enjoy honeymoon. As it is rightly said, "Those who desire honey must be ready to boldly travel down sacrifice Boulevard!"

The saying goes: "What an old man can see, a young man cannot; even if he climbs a tree." Let the old man in the spirit (Holy Spirit) guide you to good judgment and find a way out.

THE WAY OUT

1. Bad dreams are horrible and are loaded with disaster. For this reason, don't joke with dream, belief something is about to happen that is why God reveals it to you in your sleep.
2. You are advised to go for deliverance so that you may not be a stone cast aside.
3. Be a prayer warrior and a prayer warlord. Let your prayer scatter powers of darkness troubling your destiny.
4. When you are in doubt of a dream, go for counsel in a living church that knows how to go about it.
5. Always cover yourself, your property and environment with blood of Jesus.

6. Be a born again Christian in and out. Let sin be far from you, and be far from sin as well. Conquer sin and revolt against it in your heart and in behaviour.

7. Pray for smooth flow journey of life.

8. Pray and pull down every barrier against your destiny.

9. Pray for divine driver and mechanic that will navigate the vehicle of your life to Promised Land.

10. Pray for wind of change to locate you.

11. Pray without ceasing. Stop provocative act of witchcraft, lawlessness, and criminal manipulation in the dream.

12. Ask for grace and mercy of God upon your life.

13. Read the Bible. It is a book that reveals wholesome power of God for protection and deliverance.

14. Read good Christian books that liberate souls from captivity of Satan.

BIBLICAL GUIDELINE

1. Bible Reading: Exodus 14.

2. Bible Reference: Matthew 21:1-2.

1. ***"And when they drew right unto Jerusalem, and were come to Bethphage, unto the mount of Olives, then sent Jesus two disciples.***
2. ***Saying unto them, Go into the village over against you and straightway ye shall find an ass tied, and a colt with her: loose them, and bring them unto me."***
3. Positive Confession: Luke 1:37.

   "For with God nothing shall be impossible."
4. Champion Prayer: Every impossibility in my life become possible, in the name of Jesus.
5. Fasting: 6am-6pm.
6. Time of Prayer: 12pm-3am.
7. Duration of Prayer: 7 days fasting and prayer.

PRAYER POINTS

1. O Lord, let my calling\business blossom in the name of Jesus.
2. Where others fail, I shall triumph in the name of Jesus.
3. Any power assign to adulterate the honey of my life, die in the name of Jesus.
4. Every disaster that harbor itself in my dream, scatter in the name of Jesus.

5. O Lord, fire arrow and scatter powers troubling my destiny.

6. Dark powers hunting me about, die, in the name of Jesus.

7. Every stubborn pursuer in my life summersault and die, in the name of Jesus.

8. Dark chariot hired to pursue me catch fire and roast to ashes in the name of Jesus.

9. Riders of dark chariot against my life, summersault and die, in the name of Jesus.

10. Dark padlock fashioned against my calling, break in the name of Jesus.

11. Every power marching after me perish in the Red Sea in the name of Jesus.

12. O Lord, make me to stand firm to see your salvation, in the name of Jesus.

13. Thou staff of God in my hand, divide my Red Sea, in the order of Moses, in the name of Jesus.

14. Thou angel of God, lead me in my ministry, in the name of Jesus.

15. Pillar of cloud stay between me and my enemy, until I succeed in the name of Jesus.

16. Blood of Jesus, heal my ministry in the name of Jesus.

17. Blood of Jesus, flow from my head to my toe, for fresh anointing.

18. Blood of Jesus, clear way for me to excel in the name of Jesus.
19. I drink blood of Jesus, to energize and give me hope in the name of Jesus.
20. I fumigate my ministry and environ with blood of Jesus against demonic pesticides.
21. Blood of Jesus, make room for me to swim in you.
22. I pull down every barrier against my destiny in the name of Jesus.
23. I pull down every barrier against my calling in the name of Jesus.
24. I pull down every barrier against my home in the name of Jesus.
25. Lord Jesus, put right spanner into the vehicle of my ministry, in the name of Jesus.
26. Lord Jesus, be the driver of my ministry's vehicle in the name of Jesus.
27. Lord Jesus, let wind of change blow in my ministry in the name of Jesus.
28. Wind of change of financial breakthrough move in my ministry.
29. Witchcraft gathering against my ministry, scatter in the name of Jesus.
30. Witchcraft gathering against my calling, scatter in the name of Jesus.

31. Negative gathering in my ministry scatter in the name of Jesus.

32. Arrow of confusion fired against my ministry, backfire in the name of Jesus.

33. Every heart hardened against my ministry melt in the name of Jesus.

34. Thou strong east wind blow, and let my dry ground appear for me to occupy my Canaan land.

35. Let my enemy sink to the depth of sea like a stone in the name of Jesus.

36. Angels of God, slap and disgrace those that oppose me in the name of Jesus.

37. O Lord, use your right hand to shatter my enemy in the name of Jesus.

38. O Lord, use your right hand to scatter my enemy in the name of Jesus.

39. Angels of God, draw your sword against my enemy, in the name of Jesus.

40. Wheels of evil chariot pull out, and stop by fire from pursing me, in the name of Jesus.

41. O Lord, let my enemy melt away, in the name of Jesus.

42. O Lord, let terror and dread fall upon dark powers assign against my ministry.

43. Buyers and sellers that turns my ministry to buying and selling avenue instead of house of prayer I flog you out.

44. Lord Jesus, let arrow of waste leaves my life.

45. Healing power, find foundation in my ministry in the name of Jesus.

46. Power to save and deliver occupy my ministry in the name of Jesus.

47. Every dark tree assign against my ministry wither to your root in the name of Jesus.

48. Arrow of impossibility fired against my life backfire, in the name of Jesus.

49. Arrow of un-seriousness fired against my life backfire, in the name of Jesus.

50. Any power that change mind in order to attack me, shall fail in the name of Jesus.

51. I shall not be a servant to any slave master in the dream in the name of Jesus.

52. I shall not fear before enemies in the name of Jesus.

53. I shall not die before my time in the name of Jesus.

54. I walk out of captivity, and occupy my Promised Land, in the name of Jesus.

55. My Lord shall fight for me and shall see my enemy no more, in the name of Jesus.

56. O Lord, give me glory over my enemies in the name of Jesus.

57. O Lord my God, redeem me and promote me in the name of Jesus.

58. O Lord, break every yoke upon my ministry in the name of Jesus.

59. My buried potentials be exhumed in the name of Jesus.

60. Armies of heaven, take control of my ministry in the name of Jesus.

61. Powers that swallow prayer in my ministry die in the name of Jesus.

62. O Lord, guide me and make me secure special place you have for me, in the name of Jesus.

63. Hosanna in the highest! Shall rent air in my ministry in the name of Jesus.

64. I shall ride with King of kings in my ministry in the name of Jesus.

65. My ministry shall experience triumphant journey in the name of Jesus.

66. Rain of breakthrough fall upon my ministry, in the name of Jesus.

YOU HAVE BATTLES TO WIN
TRY THESE BOOKS

1. COMMAND THE DAY: DAILY PRAYER BOOK

Each day of the week is loaded with meanings and divine assurance. God did not create each day of the week for the fun of it. Blessings, success, gifts, resources, hopes, portfolios, duties, rights, prophecies, warnings and challenges, are loaded in each day.

Do you know the language, command or decree you can use to claim what belongs to you in each day of the week? Do you know in Christendom, Monday can be equated to one of the days of creation in Genesis chapter one? Do you know creation lasted for six days and God rested on the seventh day? What day of the week can Christian equate as the first day of the week, if we follow Christian calendar? What day can we call day seven?

This book shall give insight to these questions. It shall explain how you can command each day of the week according to creation in the book of Genesis chapter one.

Above all, you shall exercise your right and claim what is hidden in each day of the week.
Check for this in COMMAND THE DAY: DAILY PRAYER BOOK

2. PRAYER TO REMEMBER DREAMS

A lot of people are passing through this spiritual epidemic on a daily basis. Their dream life is epileptic, having no ability to remember all dreams they dream, or sometimes forget everything entirely. This is nothing but spiritual havoc you need to erase from your spiritual record.
The answer to every form of spiritual blackout caused by spiritual erasers is found in, PRAYER TO REMEMBER DREAMS

3. 100% CONFESSIONS AND PROPHECIES TO LOCATE HELPERS AND HELPERS TO LOCATE YOU

This is a wonderful book on confessions and prophecies to locate helpers and helpers to locate you. It is a prayer book loaded with over two thousand (2,000) prayer points.

The book unravels how to locate unknown helpers, prayers to arrest mind of helpers and prayers for manifestation after encounter with helpers.

4. ANOINTING FOR ELEVENTH HOUR HELP: HOPE AND HELP FOR YOUR TURBULENT TIMES

This book tells much of what to do at injury hour called eleventh hour. When you read and use this book as prescribed fear shall vanish in your life when pursuing a project, career or contract.

5. PRAYER TO LOCATE HELPERS AND HELPERS TO LOCATE YOU

Our divine helper is God. He created us to be together and be of help to one another. In the midst of no help we lost out, ending our journey in the wilderness.

There are keys assign to open right doors of life. You need right key to locate your helpers. Enough is enough; of suffering in silence.

With this book, you shall locate your helpers while your helpers shall locate you.

6. FIRE FOR FIRE PART ONE: (PRAYER BOOK BOOK 1)

This prayer book is fast at answering spiritual problems. It is a bulldozer prayer book, full of prayers all through. It is highly recommended for night vigil. Testimonies are pouring in daily from users of this book across the world!

7. PRAYER FOR FRUIT OF THE WOMB: EXPECTING MOTHERS

This prayer book is children magnet. By faith and believe in God Almighty, as soon as you use this book open doors to child bearing shall be yours. Amen

8. PRAYER FOR PREGNANT WOMEN: WITH ALL CHRISTIAN NAMES AND MEANINGS

This is a spiritual prayer book loaded with prayers of solution for pregnant women. As soon as you take in, the prayers you shall pray from day one of conception to the day of delivery are written in this book.

9. <u>WARFARE IN THE OFFICE: PRAYER TO SILENCE TOUGH TIMES IN OFFICE</u>

It is high time you pray prayers of power must change hands in office. Use this book and liberate yourself from every form of office yoke.

10. <u>MY MARRIAGE SHALL NOT BREAK: THE SECRET TO LOVE AND MARRIAGE THAT LASTS</u>

Marriage is corner piece of life, happiness and joy. You need to hold it tight and guide it from wicked intruders and destroyer of homes.

11. <u>VICTORY OVER SATANIC HOUSE PART ONE: RIDDING YOUR HOME OF SPIRITUAL DARKNESS</u>

Are you a tenant, Land lord bombarded left and right, front and back by wicked people around you?
With this book you shall be liberated from the hooks of the enemy.

12. <u>DICTIONARY OF DREAMS: THE DREAM INTERPRETATION</u>

DICTIONARY WITH SYMBOLS, SIGNS, AND MEANINGS

This is a must book for every home. It gives accurate details to about **10,000 (Ten thousand) dreams and interpretations,** written in alphabetical order for quick reference and easy digestion. The book portrays spiritual revelations with sound prophetic guidelines. It is loaded with Biblical references and violent prayers.

Ask for yours today.

For Further Enquiries Contact
THE AUTHOR
EVANGELIST TELLA OLAYERI
P.O. Box 1872 Shomolu Lagos.
Tel: 08023583168

FROM AUTHOR'S DESK

BEFORE YOU GO

Hello,

Thank you for purchasing this book. Would you consider posting a review about this book? In addition to providing feedback and arousing others into Christ's bosom, reviews can help other customers to know about the book.

Please take a minute to leave a review on this book.

I would appreciate that!

Thank you in advance, for your review and your patronage!!

Feel free to drop us your prayer request. We will join faith with you and God's power will be released in your life and issue in question.

http://tellaolaveri.com/prayerrequest.php

NOTE: You can get all my books from my website http://tellaolaveri.com

GOOD NEWS!!!

My audiobook is now available, to get one visit acx.com and search **"Tella Olayeri."**

Brethren, to be loaded and reloaded visit: amazon.com/author/tellaolayeri for a full spiritual sojourn for my books.

Thanks.